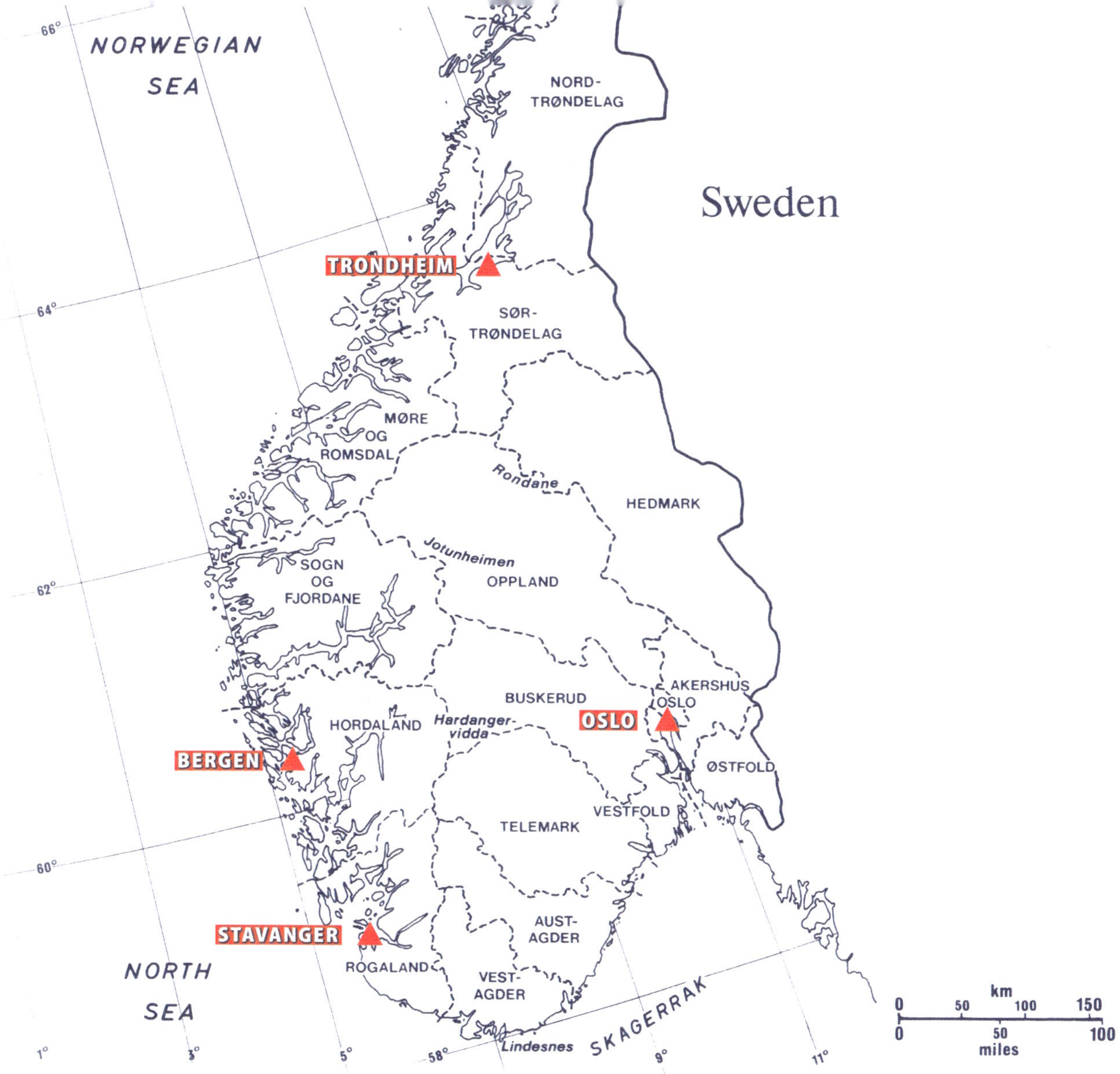
NORWEGIAN SEA
NORD-TRØNDELAG
Sweden
TRONDHEIM
SØR-TRØNDELAG
MØRE OG ROMSDAL
Rondane
HEDMARK
Jotunheimen
OPPLAND
SOGN OG FJORDANE
AKERSHUS
OSLO
BUSKERUD
HORDALAND
Hardanger-vidda
OSLO
BERGEN
ØSTFOLD
VESTFOLD
TELEMARK
STAVANGER
AUST-AGDER
ROGALAND
VEST-AGDER
NORTH SEA
Lindesnes
SKAGERRAK
66°
64°
62°
60°
58°
1°
3°
5°
9°
11°
km
0
50
100
150
0
50
100
miles

Bunads in America: A Norwegian Cultural Tradition in Southern California

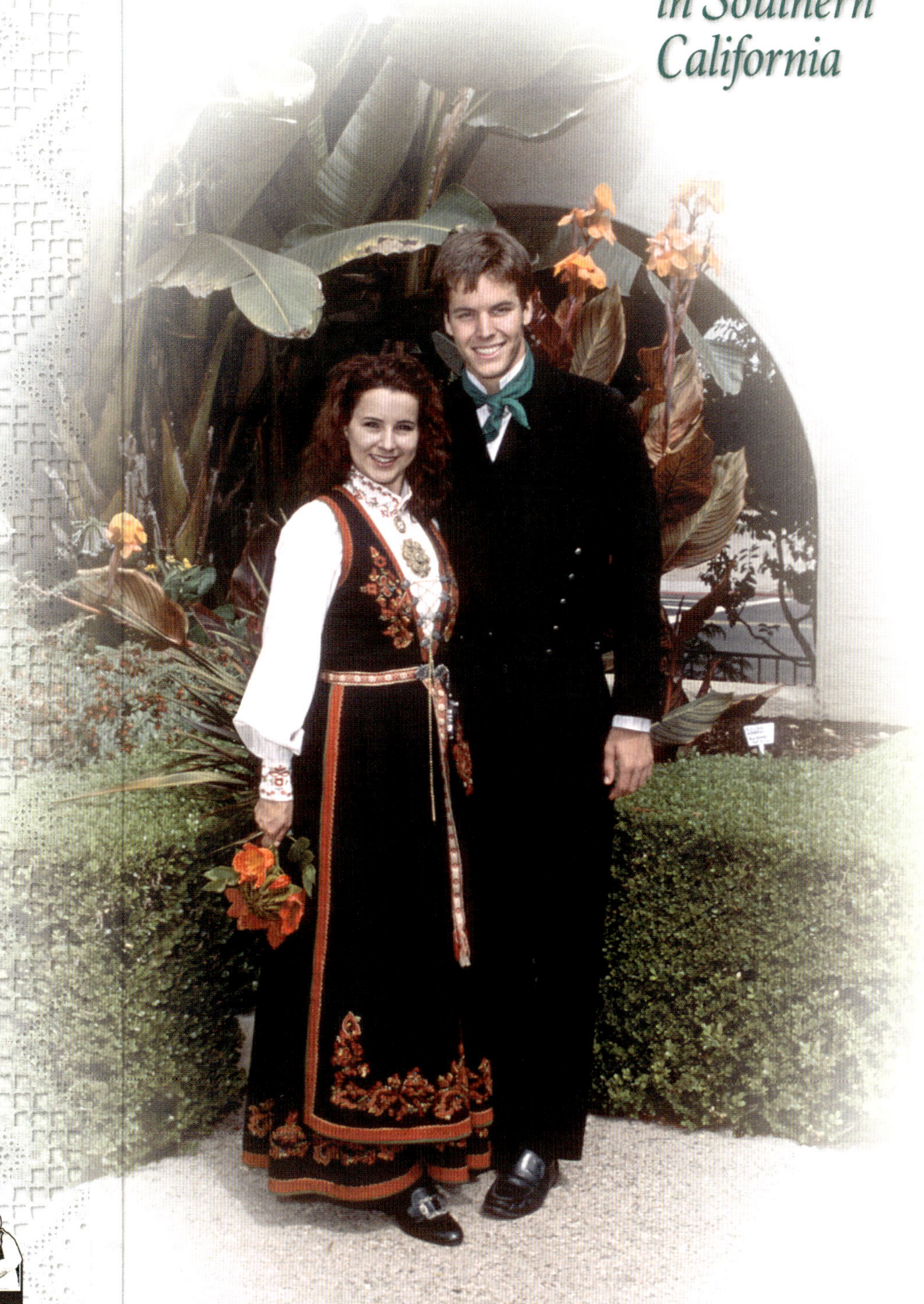

Anne Kløvnes Høidal

LADIES OF VALHALL
5740 Lance Street
San Diego, CA 92120

ISBN 0-9724138-0-4

Designed by David J. Boe.

The author is grateful for permission to photograph antique jewelry, costumes and accessories shown throughout the book.

The author is grateful for permission to reprint old family photographs from the following sources. Scanning, retouching and restoration by David J. Boe.

Serine Oline Heitlo, pg. 12, provided by Dale Roybal; married woman in Fana bunad, pg. 14, and folk dancers from Fana, pg. 16, provided by Esther Dyer; Birgit Nilsdatter Skjervheim, pg. 18, provided by Bjørn Sandelien; Farmers' trade association, pg. 24, Lise Halvorsen, pg. 26 and four young women in Fana bunads, pg. 30, provided by Esther Dyer; Marta and Endre Seim, pg. 28, provided by Thorbjørn and Kari Gjerde; Mari Sandelien, Mari and Engebret Sahl, pg. 32, provided by Bjørn Sandelien.

Acknowledgements

The road that led to ***Bunads in America: A Norwegian Cultural Tradition in Southern California*** is in many ways unique because so many people have joined me on the journey. Without the participation of the local community in providing information, money and encouragement, this book would never have materialized. The book therefore belongs to all who came forward with their support and encouragement. To all my old friends, and to the many new ones I made in the process, I would like to express my gratitude and thanks. You were great company on the road!

The first to give me encouragement for my ideas, and later also very generous financial backing, was my "own group," the Ladies of Valhall, Valhall Lodge #25, Sons of Norway, San Diego. Their support has been absolutely unwavering and therefore a moral booster of great value. Out of this group, six ladies formed a Bunad Committee. They are: Mary Fry, Ingrid Lindgren, Lizzie Riiber, Tamara Stautland, Lorraine Tucker, and Centes Wheeler. They have helped me collect the necessary data in the Norwegian-American community, provided me with much needed help during photo sessions, as well as letting others borrow from their personal store of silver and garments so the pictures could be as correct as possible. They have also given me advice and encouragement at every turn of the project. Lizzie Riiber and Dale Roybal in addition provided several participants in the bunad project with very valuable information and helped them in the acquisition and sewing of several costumes. This enriched a very lively cultural setting for the project.

Another early sponsorship for the book came from the Norwegian Information Service in New York, led by Consul Lars Fure. The Information Service's monetary support and belief in the project was of tremendous value. The major backing we received from Valhall Corporation, Valhall Lodge #25, was a decisive factor in our successful fundraising. Other organizations which generously have given us financial support are the Sons of Norway Foundation, the Norwegian Fish Club of San Diego, and the House of Norway, which also opened its cottage for our use during photo sessions in Balboa Park. Mrs. Charlotte Nielsen through the Nielsen Survivors Trust and Mrs. Audrey Geisel through the Dr. Seuss Foundation also donated very generously to the book project. Husfliden in Ålesund has supported us both monetarily and by providing information about hard to identify costumes from Sunnmøre.

We are very much obliged to Lael, Karolyn and Annika Kovtun for their splendid benefit luncheon for the book project. Jay and Lael Kovtun very graciously opened their beautiful home for the luncheon. The financial support this event generated was very important, and the enjoyment the guests received in return for their support was a precious gift in itself. Both Annika and Lael have also contributed to the project by modeling some of the costumes pictured in the book.

Several individuals have sponsored the book project in a major way. They are: Greta Berg, Esther Dyer, Mary Fry, Glen and Carmen Hagen, Edvard and Barbara Hemmingsen, Adolf and Mary Jacobsen, Ole Josoy and his granddaughter, Hanna Marie, Erling and Vernette Karlsgodt, Helga Moore, Virginia Napierskie, Inger S. Olson, Dale Roybal, Alan Sczepaniak and Helen Seiler. Many other individuals who are listed in the book have also supported us very enthusiastically, for which we are very grateful.

There are also a number of persons who unselfishly have given of their time and resources. David Boe, the coordinator of the book, has used countless hours of work on the project. His professional knowledge has been of great value, and his advice and friendship have been of equal value. Without his generous contribution, this book would have looked very different. Photographer Ed Schaffroth has worked very hard to illustrate the book. Without his dedication and very minimal fee, the project could not have been completed in the way it has been done. Another photographer, Bernt Erik Nilsen, provided us with a great *con amore* service for the book by taking the pictures of the antique jewelry and the old costume pieces. Marlene Lesney and Tamara Stautland have very graciously proofread the manuscript, as has my husband, Oddvar K. Høidal. His advice and encouragement has been essential for me. My husband's cousin, Gerd Høydalsvik of Ørsta, Norway, was very helpful in providing information and reading a portion of the manuscript.

Anne Kløvnes Høidal *San Diego, December 2001*

The Bunad Committee, Ladies of Valhall

***Front row** (from left): Tamara Tow Stautland (Silje), Ingrid Bårdseng Lindgren (Rondastakk), Lizzie Skyllstad Riiber (Sunnmøre), and Lorraine Reinholdtsen Tucker (Bergen). **Back row:** Centes Kjensrud Wheeler (Valdres), Anne Kløvnes Høidal (Nordland), and Mary Otto Fry (North Hallingdal).*

***Rear view** (from left): Lizzie Skyllstad Riiber, Ingrid Bårdseng Lindgren, Tamara Tow Stautland, Anne Kløvnes Høidal, Centes Kjensrud Wheeler, Mary Otto Fry, and Lorraine Reinholdtsen Tucker.*

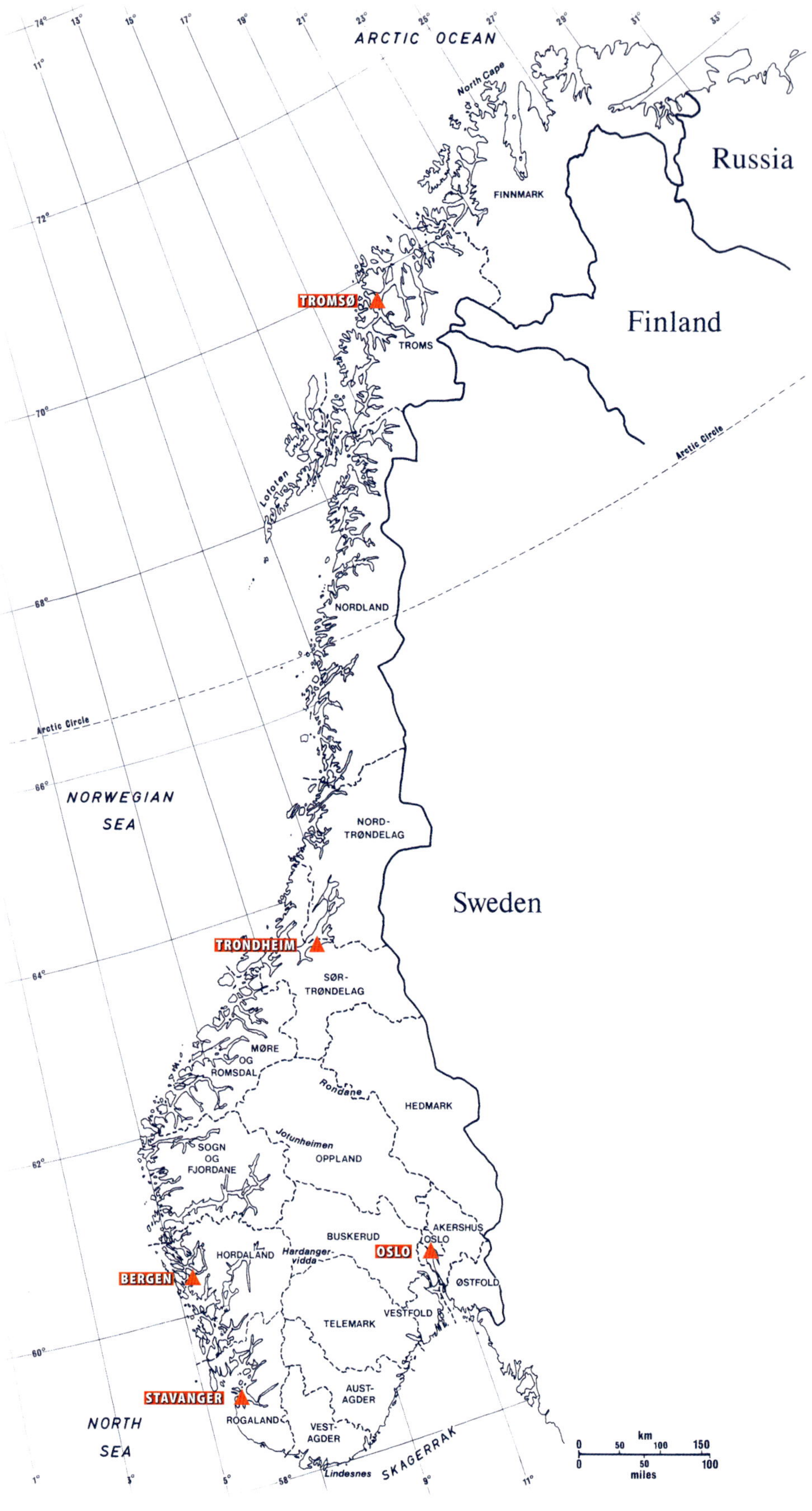

ARCTIC OCEAN
North Cape
Russia
FINNMARK
Finland
TROMSØ
TROMS
Lofoten
Arctic Circle
NORDLAND
NORWEGIAN
SEA
NORD-
TRØNDELAG
Sweden
TRONDHEIM
SØR-
TRØNDELAG
MØRE
OG
ROMSDAL
Rondane
HEDMARK
Jotunheimen
SOGN
OG
FJORDANE
OPPLAND
BUSKERUD
AKERSHUS
OSLO
HORDALAND
Hardanger-
vidda
BERGEN
ØSTFOLD
TELEMARK
VESTFOLD
STAVANGER
AUST-
AGDER
ROGALAND
VEST-
AGDER
NORTH
SEA
Lindesnes
SKAGERRAK
km
0 50 100 150
0 50 100
miles

Contents

Purpose of the Bunad Project

TOP OF PAGE: Belt for Hardanger bunad, worn by Birgit Sahl Otto. Contributed by Mary Fry, Birgit's daughter.

EVERY 17TH OF MAY the Norwegian-American community in Southern California goes into high gear. Each year there are several celebrations of the day, ranging from fancy galas to flag-raising ceremonies. It is certainly a time to dust off your bunad and show your colors! And each year I have been impressed by the variety of bunads and the pride people show in their Norwegian heritage. Like in Norway, there is an upsurge of interest for the bunad tradition in Southern California, and at present quite a few in our community are in the process of acquiring a new bunad.

Perhaps it might be of interest to know how many persons already own a bunad or festdrakt in our community. As an example, I would like to use Valhall Lodge # 25 of Sons of Norway in San Diego. In January 2000 the membership list consisted of 345 members. Of these, 196 were women, approximately 57%. There was only one man with a bunad, but 55 women. Children's bunads were not counted since they are not individual members of the Lodge. This means 28% of the women have a bunad or festdrakt, and quite a few more than one. There are also many who have interesting parts of old costumes. As an example, it can be mentioned that a particular man's shirt is said to be 200 years old!

As already mentioned, quite a number of individuals are in the process of acquiring a new bunad, which indicates that the bunad "wave" in Norway is having a ripple effect all the way to Southern California. For the Norwegian-American community in Southern California, this is important. An increased awareness of our cultural roots and strong ties to Norway are what will preserve our Norwegian-American identity and love for our rich cultural heritage.

The bunad tradition is of course just a part of this Norwegian cultural heritage, but a very visible one. When wearing a bunad, you feel like a representative of Norway and your Norwegian roots. And what a representative! A woman in a complete and well-made bunad is like a sailing ship with all sails flying — a beautiful sight!

While working on this project, I have encountered many questions pertaining to our bunad tradition, as well as practical questions such as how to go about purchasing a bunad, what is the correct bunad for me, or how to care for a bunad. This indicates that there is a great need for more information, and how to find such information. Chapters III and IV are meant to answer some of these questions.

Chapter I on the Norwegian bunad tradition is meant among other things to make people aware of the strong local tradition most bunads have in Norway. It is hoped that this will encourage people to do some research before buying a new bunad and perhaps avoid pitfalls, including buying less than authentic "kits" which are available for purchase, or making up a "look-alike" costume on their own.

The major part of this publication is devoted to providing information about the different bunads and festdrakts which exist in our community. A commentary on each costume will precede individual stories about the owners and their particular outfit. In this way, people will recognize others in their community who own a bunad from their own "home" area in Norway and have a chance to contact these persons to study their costumes. It is also important to have a record of this particular part of our Norwegian culture at the beginning of the third millennium.

It has been very interesting to see what kind of bunads and festdrakts exist in our area, what parts of Norway are represented, and how the owners have acquired their costumes. It may also be of interest to compare the acquisitions of the last few years with those which have been in use earlier. As mentioned, there is a trend brewing. There are very few men in Southern California with a bunad. This is very regrettable, but may slowly change. Several men have shown interest in acquiring a costume. Perhaps the increasing trend among men in Norway to wear bunads will have an impact on men in Southern California as well. Bunads among women are popular, both among the young and those who are older. It has been very interesting to note that the newer acquisitions have in large part consisted of very traditional costumes, well made and based on family connections to a particular bunad area in Norway. Most people are also increasingly aware of the importance of obtaining the correct shirt and shoes for their bunad, something which previously was not always the case.

CHAPTER I

The Bunad Tradition in Norway

Early in the nineteenth century foreign visitors to Norway noticed that people living in Oslo and other Norwegian towns dressed much like their counterparts in the rest of Europe. The fashions were basically dictated by trends in London and Paris. Imported fashion magazines were studied, and local seamstresses did a very good job copying the latest innovations. Some people, especially among the wealthy, were also able to import clothing directly from abroad, and these items were most likely scrutinized carefully and copied by their contemporaries.

...each type of folk costume had its own history of development, distinct from the upper class fashion trend, yet influenced by it in varying degrees.

Foreign observers also noticed that city fashions were spreading along the main highways. The first people in the countryside to adopt new trends were the more well to do. Some imported materials were already in use before 1800. We notice this in particular in coastal areas with some wealth and connections with the outside world. The influence of imported materials was especially noteworthy along the southern and western seaboards, where shipping connections with England and the continent were strong.

European fashions had a single developing history; more or less specific to each region we look at. This was different from the way folk costumes developed during the same time period. They included — in one and the same period — many different trends, which varied from one country to another, as well as within each country. Here each type of folk costume had its own history of development, distinct from the upper class fashion trend, yet influenced by it in varying degrees.

So how do we define the term folk costume. Folk costumes were clothing which had local characteristics, and which were used in different villages in the countryside. There were several gradations between clothing for work and festive attire. For example, in Norway it was practically unthinkable to wear an everyday outfit to church.

TOP OF PAGE: Married woman's belt from Voss. Gilt silver ornaments from 1836-37. From Thorbjørn Gjerde's family.

The term bunad is used about a costume which to a greater or lesser degree is a revival of a local folk costume tradition. A bunad comes in addition to our regular modern day clothing, and is very different from such.

There were set rules for how and when to use different parts of the costumes. This very rich heritage became simplified over the years. For instance, the difference in costumes for married and unmarried women disappeared in many communities. Certain pieces of clothing which were used only in church, like the Hallingdal woman's apron, later became part of the festive attire any time it was used. On the other hand, the jackets for women were worn much less than before. It used to be unthinkable both for men and women to go to church without a jacket, no matter how warm it was. You were more properly dressed with a jacket, and that was the deciding factor, not the temperature.

The almost hundred-year-old term bunad may need some clarification to show the difference between folk costumes and bunads. The term bunad is used about a costume which to a greater or lesser degree is a revival of a local folk costume tradition. A bunad comes in addition to our regular modern day clothing, and is very different from such. The use of the bunad is a conscious attempt to carry on or to revive an old tradition. Bunads in this sense of the word have been in use for more than 100 years.

Compared to the old folk costumes, the modern costumes or bunads have much less individuality in their use of colors and

Serine Oline Heitlo from Verdal in a Hardanger bunad, 1916. Contributed by Dale Roybal, Serine's granddaughter.

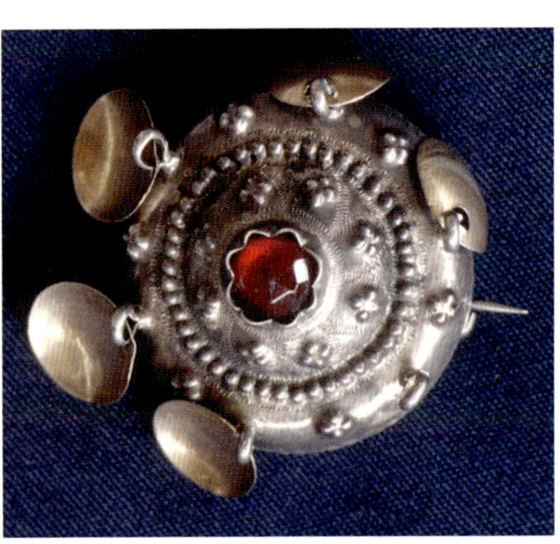

Over 100 years old sølje from Hardanger. Contributed by Hulda Velken.

decorations. The end result of this has been a standardized attire made for all festive occasions. In the folk costume tradition there were of course clothes both for work and for festive occasions. Clothing which was worn for holidays and feasts were more expensive and therefore better taken care of than other garments. Consequently these were preserved longer. This is the reason that museums have so many festive outfits compared to work clothes. The modern bunad is also used only for special occasions, so it is natural that it builds on and preserves the old tradition for festive attire. We just have to remember that our festive bunads were not what people wore every day.

Clothing which was worn for holidays and feasts were more expensive and therefore better taken care of than other garments. Consequently these were preserved longer.

From the early 19th century, local traditions in the Norwegian countryside were losing ground to European city fashions. This development increased rapidly after factory produced clothing made its way into the country at the end of the century. Men were in general the first to abandon their folk costumes. In some areas, however, the local clothing tradition survived in full or partial use into the 20th century and even up to World War II. If we include the Sami folk costume, as we ought to, we can say it is still worn on a daily basis. On the whole, folk costume traditions in Norway survived much longer than in other European countries.

Bodice insert for Hardanger costume from Disa Jordal Årtun, Myrtle Whitworth's mother, born 1894.

In some areas of Norway we find a very strong living folk costume tradition, with Setesdal, Valdres, Hallingdal, Telemark, Fana by Bergen, Hardanger, Voss, Røros and Gudbrandsdalen being the best known districts.

In some areas of Norway we find a very strong living folk costume tradition, with Setesdal, Valdres, Hallingdal, Telemark, Fana by Bergen, Hardanger, Voss, Røros and Gudbrandsdalen being the best known districts. In these areas there has been continual use of the old costumes at least for festive occasions, and in some places people dressed in traditional costumes for everyday use as well up until World War II. Setesdal is a good example of this, and in Bø, in Telemark, a few women were still wearing their everyday costumes as late as 1988.

The last half of the 19th century was a period in Norwegian history when it became important to build a national identity. This trend, which is called the national Romantic Movement, was not uniquely Norwegian, but perhaps became more important in Norway than in most other European countries. To understand this, we have to remember Norway's political situation at the time. The country was in a very unequal union with Sweden, which had been forced upon the nation in 1814. Ever since this union the Norwegian government, as well as the people as a whole, had struggled for greater independence and recognition of a growing awareness of being a separate nation. Consequently, increased interest evolved for Norwegian architecture, furniture, folk costumes, folk music and dances, as well as

Married woman in a Fana bunad, 1904. Contributed by Esther Dyer.

Vestlandssølje with masks behind the disks, ca. 1900. Contributed by Lizzie Riiber.

for fairy tales. This is very well illustrated in the many interesting paintings that appeared at this time. For most of us the well-known painting "The Bridal Party in Hardanger" by Tiedeman and Gude (1848) is familiar and can serve as an illustration. The fact that this painting became so admired by the Christiania (Oslo) bourgeoisie that a tableau of it was arranged at an evening entertainment may be less well known. The leading young ladies and gentlemen in society dressed up in folk costumes and enacted the event depicted in the painting. Folk music was also performed.

This period of national Romanticism became a time in Norwegian history when it was important to strengthen national identity. The peasant culture was viewed as something valuable and uniquely Norwegian, something which one could build upon and develop further. As part of this, interest in national costumes occurred and grew stronger over the years. So instead of regarding the peasants coming to town in their folk costumes as quaint or even ugly and unrefined, a new positive attitude emerged among the upper classes. The costumes became "interesting" and an expression of the Norwegian national spirit. Some ladies even acquired a costume, perhaps because of a desire to show a national attitude, or perhaps the costumes were deemed flattering and different.

This period of national Romanticism became a time in Norwegian history when it was important to strengthen national identity. As part of this, interest in national costumes occurred and grew stronger over the years.

Old wood carving, pendant on chain. Contributed by Hulda Velken.

Hulda Garborg… was the one who coined the term bunad, meaning a costume based on the old folk costume tradition.

At the beginning of the 20th century there was a broader upsurge in interest for the old Norwegian folk costumes. People who worked to revive old folk dances also spearheaded the effort to preserve the folk costume tradition. Hulda Garborg was a very influential person in this regard. She was the one who coined the term bunad, meaning a costume based on the old folk costume tradition. Without her enormous effort and influence much of the folk traditions would have been lost, especially with regards to the folk dances and the wearing of bunads. She studied folk dances and started many folk dance groups. And what could be more natural than to have the dancers dress in folk costumes. For Hulda Garborg it was important that the costumes should be practical for dancing, look attractive and be "Norwegian." To achieve this, she started a trend that has lasted up until our time. She stressed that the fabrics should be produced in Norway. She preferred a costume with a fitted bodice, and emphasized wool embroidery on the skirt, bodice, pocket or purse, and cap. If there were no precedence for embroidery on a costume, a pattern could be copied from *rosemaling* (rose painting) on chests or cupboards, or from an existing embroidered cap or shawl. This fashion also came to districts that had an old, rich and still living tradition. In these areas the old tradition and

Anna and Jon Fanavold, Olivia Olsen and Andreas Simonsen, folk dancers from Fana, ca. 1900. Contributed by Esther Dyer.

the new ideas often lived side by side. The heavy emphasis on embroidery, however, created ideals which many folk costumes never had.

For Hulda Garborg it was important that the costumes should be practical for dancing, look attractive and be "Norwegian."

Gradually a change occurred. People recognized that imported fabrics had been an integral part of many folk costumes for a very long time. Costumes in some places had little or no embroidery at all. In our own time more extensive research has been done, and there has been a very conscious effort to recreate the old original folk costumes or to get as close to the originals as possible.

This new trend has created great diversity. Around 1900 the Hardanger bunad was greatly admired and became our first "national costume." It was worn all over Norway as a national costume, in cities as well as in the countryside, even in areas that had their own costume tradition. Queen Maud was given a Hardanger costume and was photographed in it. The Hallingdal costume, revised by Hulda Garborg, also became popular as a "national costume," but never gained the widespread popularity of the Hardanger bunad.

Today the trend in the bunad tradition is two-pronged. The main trend goes toward revising old existing bunads so they come closer to the original folk costumes, or new costumes are reconstructed based on a great deal of research and new source material.

Shirt insert for Voss winter bunad (1920's). Sølje (1905) from Gjørid Songve, Kari Gjerde's mother. Contributed by Kari Gjerde.

The ideal is also that a bunad should be a representative copy of a particular folk costume from a distinct area within a specific period of time.

Old costumes, or most often parts of costumes, are dug out of chests and drawers. The ideal is also that a bunad should be a representative copy of a particular folk costume from a distinct area within a specific period of time. When speaking of folk costumes, an area is described or considered to be a separate area when it has its own costume tradition, which distinguishes it from other districts and from city fashions at the same time. The costume or bunad should be reconstructed according to a local costume tradition. Exact copies are for many obvious reasons not always possible. When reconstructing a costume, attention is also paid to what time period a costume belongs. Garments from different time periods cannot, for example, be combined. The different variations or results of the reconstructions will be discussed later, but the variety of new reconstructed costumes is increasing every year.

The second trend is represented by the many festdrakts or festive attires. Most of them are based on the cut of old folk costumes, but not necessarily from their own district. Many of them have little direct connection with any specific folk costume area or time period. Most festdrakts are heavily embroidered, inspired by local nature or history. These costumes are sometimes somewhat less expensive to buy than many traditional bunads and are therefore

Old filigree cuff links. Inherited by Lizzie Riiber from her great grandfather (born 1859) from Valdres. Contributed by Lizzie Riiber.

Birgit Nilsdatter Skjervheim (1846-1920) from Hallingdal, Mary Fry's great grandmother. Contributed by Bjørn Sandelien.

chosen for this reason. They may also seem more attractive or modern to people with little or no knowledge of bunad traditions. Another factor may also explain some of the popularity of the festdrakts. Many people, especially in the U.S., no longer have a very close connection with any particular area of Norway, and therefore the "look" becomes very important.

Most (festdrakts or festive attires)...are based on the cut of old folk costumes, but not necessarily from their own district.

Many bunads and festdrakts were created by people in areas with no living folk costume tradition, or scant resource material for recreating old costumes. Since the great upswing in the desire to own a bunad, many have wanted to have a festive attire representing their own home area. Consequently there is a great variation of backgrounds for the various bunads and festdrakts available in Norway today.

In the development of the Norwegian bunad tradition, the Norwegian Bunad and Folk Dress Board (Landsnemnda for bunadsspørsmål) has been very important. It was created in 1947 by the Department of Church and Education, which also deals with cultural matters in general. The Board's purpose was to give advice, and in the first twenty years it also gave approval of newly reconstructed bunads and revisions of old ones. The Board consisted of people with expertise in this field, and they had to be independent

Parts from an old Hardanger bunad, probably from 1910 (closeup, above), which belonged to Birgit Sahl Otto. Contributed by Mary Fry, her daughter.

In the development of the Norwegian bunad tradition, the Norwegian Bunad and Folk Dress Board (Landsnemnda for bunadsspørsmål) has been very important.

. . . the Board . . . will . . . direct and help people who are conducting research or work on bunads.

of any other organizations that might have conflicting interests.

After 1967 the Board has not used the word approval in its recommendations. It will, however, direct and help people who are conducting research or work on bunads. This is done free of charge. Today it is an advisory institution, which over the years has had a great influence in directing the development of the modern bunad tradition. It will, for instance, give an opinion on how the proposed bunad or part of a bunad harmonize with the local culture of the area it comes from. The Board may also be an invaluable source of information and assistance for anyone working with bunads in general.

From the 1920's an increasing number of people have wanted to own a bunad. It was not, however, any longer sufficient simply to be dressed in a "national costume." Since that time most people have desired to have a costume from their own home district, or from the district which they feel they belong to, either by family connection or emotionally. One can say that a person dressed in a local bunad in a way represents that area.

For many years one bunad, the Nordland bunad, represented all of the three northernmost provinces. Today there are several others to choose from if you come from the northern part of Norway.

Embroidered mittens from Hallingdahl. Submitted by House of Norway.

Other bunads represent a single province *(fylke)*, a county *(kommune)*, or a certain valley. Even some villages and towns have their own bunads, and in a few instances a family or a farm may have its own distinctive costume.

It is quite certain, as Astrid Lilleaas writes in her twelve volume work on bunads, that little Norway with 4.5 million inhabitants has many hundreds of different bunads.

Several attempts have been made to count how many different bunads there are in Norway. It has proven to be a difficult task. There are sometimes a great many variations of a bunad. As an example, it can be mentioned that in Valdres there are some checked or plaid bunads which could be counted as two or as thirty - fifteen variations for men and the same for women, which again may be varied in a number of combinations with different aprons and headgear. It is quite certain, as Astrid Lilleaas writes in her twelve volume work on bunads, that little Norway with 4.5 million inhabitants has many hundreds of different bunads.

In this multitude of bunads there obviously will be a variety of backgrounds. Some bunads have a close connection with the old folk costume tradition, whereas others are more or less free inventions with some connections to the old costumes. A useful description by the Norwegian Bunad and Folk Dress Board divides bunads into five categories:

1. Bunads which represent the last development in an old unbro-

View of back.

Vestlandssølje. *Contributed by Janice Huckins.*

Detail view.

ken folk costume tradition. In this group the old folk costumes, both for work and festive occasions, had not disappeared by the time appreciation of the folk costume tradition developed. They thereupon gained a new function as a bunad. The old bunads from Hardanger, Fana (near Bergen), Voss, Telemark, Setesdal, Hallingdal, and Numedal are all examples of bunads with roots in a strong, unbroken tradition. Obviously these costumes are very well documented.

Some bunads have a close connection with the old folk costume tradition, whereas others are more or less free inventions with some connections to the old costumes.

2. This group includes bunads based on folk costumes which went out of use, but were not forgotten. Many people still knew what they had looked like, and at the beginning of the revival period old pieces of clothing were taken into use again.
3. Bunads that are systematically reconstructed on the basis of preserved old parts of folk costumes which are from the same areas and of the same type of costume. All other sources that describe this type of costume — for instance written sources, pictures and oral traditions — are utilized in the reconstruction.
4. Bunads that are reconstructed on the basis of accidental and sparse old costume material. Parts of the costume, which there may not have been any precedence for, were recreated in the style of the recovered pieces.

Purse for Trønder bunad. Old clasp from Numedal, inherited by Helga Moore from her grandmother. Contributed by Helga Moore.

5. Bunads that partially or entirely are free compositions, or have decorative patterns from objects other than clothing.

In the old days when people still wore folk costumes as their clothing, not as bunads for festive occasions, there was within certain limitations a great variety within each district. People basically decided how they wanted to dress. But like today, there were many unwritten rules to take into account. Most people stayed on the beaten track. There were, however, a great many choices of materials, colors and decorations, limited only by availability and buying power. A person's social and economic status was much more visible in the way a person dressed than what we are used to today.

The unwritten "laws" dictated not only the way the different pieces of clothing were made, but also for what occasion they could be used.

The unwritten "laws" dictated not only the way the different pieces of clothing were made, but also for what occasion they could be used. Most people didn't want to look out of place. In many districts people had scant contact with the outside world and changing fashions. They associated mostly with others in the village, less with people from other places and of different social standing. They compared themselves first and foremost with neighbors in their immediate community. These were the persons they wanted approval from. Nevertheless, the folk costumes changed over time. They were influenced by European fashions, by costumes in neighboring districts, and by local changes in norms, standards and

Old sølje from Numedal, inherited by Helga Moore from her grandmother. Contributed by Helga Moore.

When a novelty was adopted, it was adjusted and reshaped to merge with the old in such a way that the result formed an organic whole.

ideals. There was, however, a great difference in the degree to which each individual dress or suit assimilated a new fashion. Sometimes an entire garment was adopted, at other times one or two small details were added. Thus we often find old and new features co-existing in the very same costume.

When a novelty was adopted, it was adjusted and reshaped to merge with the old in such a way that the result formed an organic whole. It was the local and individual cut and design that created the distinctive folk costumes of Norway. As one authority says of the costumes in Setesdal, Hallingdal and Valdres, there are enough local differences in cut and design to reveal plainly the district in which a costume belongs, in spite of the fact that some costumes share the same origin and have many features in common. It is thus quite impossible to mistake a girl in a Setesdal dress from one in a Hallingdal costume. What we see today in the various costumes are survivals mixed together in a colorful potpourri. The local characteristics in the folk costumes show up first and foremost in the cut and decorations, less in the choice of fabrics. Together with homemade materials, imported ones were used. In other words, not everything was locally made. Also, the same imported cloth, ribbons, aprons and scarves have been used in several different costumes.

Farmers' trade association (mjølkemesse) meeting in Bergen, 1934. Participants in Fana bunads. Contributed by Esther Dyer.

The point is that these items have been used in a variety of ways and sometimes in very different combinations.

The folk costumes reveal traits belonging to many fashions and historical time periods, perhaps even to prehistoric times. The tablet woven belt worn today in East Telemark has its counterpart in the Oseberg Viking ship find. The high waistline of the woman's costume in Telemark, Hallingdal and Setesdal may also be very old. Some bunad experts point out that in Telemark the high waistline was worn until the middle of the nineteenth century. In Setesdal and Telemark these were also used in the early 1700's. This eliminates the possibility that they developed as a result of the nineteenth century European Empire style. How far back this fashion goes in Norway is uncertain, possibly to the Middle Ages, and it may have some connection with the hypothetical "skirt with suspenders" of the Viking Age.

The tablet woven belt worn today in East Telemark has its counterpart in the Oseberg Viking ship find.

In the same way we can trace many other features of our bunads back to certain style periods, for example the Renaissance of the 1500's or the Rococo of the eighteenth century. Other characteristics again have been influenced by the Empire style of the early 1800's. As an example of Renaissance influence, Hardanger embroidery can be mentioned. This embroidery technique has its

Bride's hand covering blanket from Voss, ca. 1900. Chest from Voss, 1844. Contributed by Kari and Thorbjørn Gjerde.

roots in the Italian Renaissance. It has been used in Norway since the 17th century for altar cloths, etc. This type of embroidery is characteristic of the Hardanger bunad's narrow apron, but is also found on shirts and kerchiefs as well as other items. By the way, the narrow aprons themselves are also a Renaissance influence.

The Renaissance style was really the first fashion wave of modern times that influenced Norwegian peasant costumes.

The Renaissance style was really the first fashion wave of modern times that influenced Norwegian peasant costumes. At that time skirts and knee breeches appeared with very narrow pleating. These breeches became very popular in Europe. The fashion arrived a little late in Norway, during the 1600's, and at different time intervals in different districts. This fashion was on the whole discarded around 1800, except in Setesdal where it served as the basis for the bridegroom's costume as late as the 1820's. In many women's costumes, however, this narrow pleating technique is still very much evident. We need only take a look at the Setesdal's woman's costumes of our own time, as well as others, for example from Hordaland and Fana. Another survival from the Renaissance period is the edging on the shoulders of some of the men's long jackets in Setesdal.

The Rococo fashions of the 18th century brought several new trends. The men started wearing tight, short knee breeches and

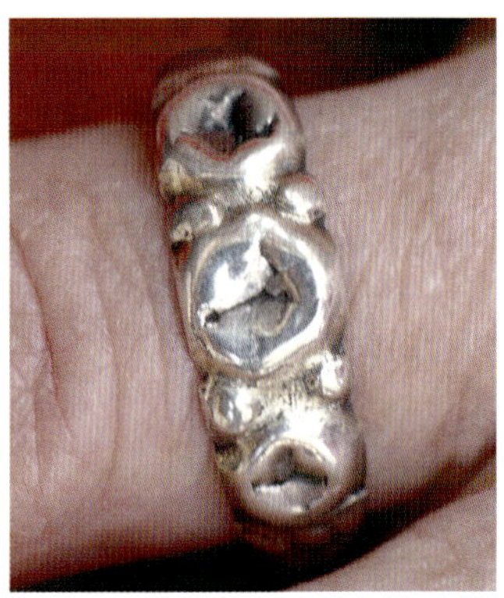

Old ring found in chest from 1781. Contributed by Lizzie Riiber.

Lise Halvorsen, Esther Dyer's aunt, in a Fana bunad, 1904. Contributed by Esther Dyer.

long waistcoats. The vest also became very popular. Sometimes up to three vests could be worn simultaneously. The innermost one was all buttoned up, whereas the next two remained open to show off this wealth of fine clothing. At this time buttons of pewter or silver and buttonholes became fashionable. Clasps and hooks had held earlier garments together. These Rococo features live on in many of our bunads. For women a wide skirt with deep pleats with an apron and a fichu or neckerchief became popular, together with a longer jacket with a fitted waist.

During the 19th century Empire period in Europe, both coats and waistcoats became shorter, while the trousers were made longer. The short coats or jackets sometimes became extremely short, like in Setesdal and Telemark, and in addition they were outfitted with high stand-up collars. The short knee breeches from the previous fashion trend survived in the folk costumes in quite a few places. The stockings for some men's outfits became embroidered in the Empire fashion, although little of that has survived into our own times. In Hallingdal even the knee breeches became heavily embroidered like the uniforms worn by the hussars during the Napoleonic period. This development is still seen in the Hallingdal costume.

The development of stockings as we know them today is an

Old bodice insert from Voss, mounted on burlap. Contributed by Kari Gjerde.

The earliest stockings were sewn from wool cloth, sometimes with a foot, sometimes without.

interesting story. The earliest stockings were sewn from wool cloth, sometimes with a foot, sometimes without. In the wintertime woolen strips of cloth were wrapped around the feet, but in summer shoes were cushioned with straw. Knitted stockings in Europe were first made from silk, probably in the 1500's in either Italy, France or Spain. These stockings were extremely expensive and not very durable, but they nevertheless became quite popular among the very wealthy. Henry VIII once ordered eight pairs of knitted silk stockings from Spain, perhaps for one of his many weddings?

At first only men knitted, but Queen Elizabeth I of England ordered that women should be employed in the trade. By her time the demand was growing, and it was a great benefit for many women who needed some income. In Scandinavia silk stockings also became popular, and King Christian IV of Denmark-Norway (1588-1648) tried to restrict the use of such an expensive luxury as silk stockings. Few, however, had the means to buy them. Knitted wool stockings did not become popular until after 1800. Before that homespun wool cloth stockings were worn. This type of stocking was used until recently with the Setesdal woman's bunad. Today men with short bunad breeches wear a variety of knitted wool stockings. Most districts have their own individual patterns.

Wedding picture of Marta and Endre Seim, Granvin in Hardanger, 1931. Contributed by Thorbjørn and Kari Gjerde.

It may come as a surprise to many that very little underwear was worn with the old folk costumes. Underwear most likely was not common in Scandinavia during the Middle Ages, nor was it in the rest of Europe. It is not before 1600 that it appears to any degree among the upper classes. This was partly because garments, which earlier had been close fitting to the body, now became more open and divided in several pieces. The new garments for women required a white linen chemise or shirt. Linen, however, was very expensive in earlier times, and the linen shirt therefore most often was very short, reaching just down to the belt, both for men and women.

At first only men knitted, but Queen Elizabeth I of England ordered that women should be employed in the trade.

Eilert Sundt, a Norwegian sociologist, reports from about 1850 that "in Setesdal women wear a short shirt, and for everyday use only one skirt *(stakk)*, which is also short. During summer they wear no shoes or stockings, except on festive occasions. The garments therefore consist of only two pieces of clothing. There may be some women who wear undergarments, but they are few and old."

The use of underwear for women increased greatly among the upper classes during the Empire period. Dress materials of the time were often very thin and almost transparent, necessitating underwear. In the Norwegian peasant community women's underpants became more widely used after 1880, first among the wealthy, but

Vest, insert and belt from Hardanger, worn by Disa Jordal Årtun, born 1894, Myrtle Whitworth's mother. Contributed by Myrtle Whitworth.

In the Norwegian peasant community women's underpants became more widely used after 1880, first among the wealthy, but more limited among servants and poorer women in the countryside.

more limited among servants and poorer women in the countryside. On the other hand, both one and two underskirts could be worn with a costume. This of course gave considerable warmth. It was not an ideal to be thin or very slim, so the extra fullness caused by the underskirts was considered attractive.

Today unfortunately we don't see too many women wearing traditional headdresses with their bunads. This is regrettable because the headdress in many ways is the most elegant and traditional piece of the bunad. In earlier times it was a shame for a grown woman not to cover her hair. Women covered their heads both indoors and outdoors. The custom was based on religious tradition. Married women could not enter the church bareheaded. Young girls could show their hair, but they also often wore caps or a headband of some kind, and in some areas a more elaborate headdress.

It is, however, easy to understand why today so few choose to wear the head covering which is part of their bunad. Many headdresses are complicated to prepare and arrange. Many bunad wearers do not know how to prepare the most elaborate hair coverings, and in some cases the special tools required to do the job may be lacking. This may be one reason why so few choose to wear them. Another reason may be that our modern hairstyles are different

Four young women in Fana bunads, 1903 or 1904. Contributed by Esther Dyer.

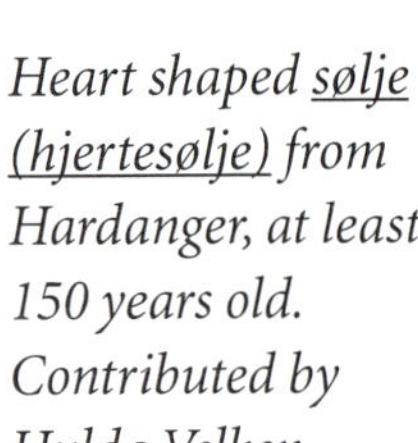

Heart shaped sølje (hjertesølje) from Hardanger, at least 150 years old. Contributed by Hulda Velken.

from the old styles with much longer hair. Aagot Noss writes that the way hair was cared for, braided and tied up didn't change much in 300 years in peasant society, and that tied up braids were the foundation which caps or other coverings were fastened to.

A considerable part of people's monetary wealth was invested in clothing and jewelry. These items were therefore an indication of people's social position as well as their wealth.

As mentioned previously, in the old days a person's clothing was more important in society than it is today. A considerable part of people's monetary wealth was invested in clothing and jewelry. These items were therefore an indication of people's social position as well as their wealth. For us today it is interesting to notice that in earlier times the official valuation of the property of a decedent's estate always mentioned clothing and jewelry, when there was any. For the wealthier people, only the most valuable clothing was enumerated and a value affixed to them. Everyday clothes were not mentioned, but divided privately among the heirs. Estates of poorer people do mention work clothes and perhaps one or two better garments, which were all distributed among the heirs by the authorities because of their importance to the survivors.

In Norwegian peasant society it was a very old tradition to acquire silver objects. There is actually a specific term for this silver, *bondesølv* (peasant silver), which includes jewelry as well as tableware owned by the farmers. Compared to farming communities in

Gilt, old søljer (bolesøljer) from Telemark. Contributed by Anne Kløvnes Høidal and Karin Brevig.

the rest of Europe, Norway seems to be in a position by itself, with Norwegian farmers on the average being both economically and socially better off than their European counterparts.

In Norwegian peasant society it was a very old tradition to acquire silver objects.

Silver jewelry, which over the years was worn with folk costumes, had its origin in imported European fashion designs, first worn in the cities by the wealthy upper class. Once this fashion was adopted among the peasants, it continued to be used long after it no longer was in vogue among the elite. Until the early 1800's all jewelry was produced in the cities, where gold and silversmiths by law had to reside. After 1839 these restrictions for the most part were lifted. Today we find silversmiths in many parts of the countryside, often specializing in bunad silver.

Erich Pontoppidan, bishop of Bergen, wrote in 1752 that women wore finger rings, which had small rings attached. These rings made a tinkling sound that "gave esteem." When we look at old costume silver, it is remarkable how much of it has tinkling attachments. It was also believed that silver provided protection against evil, therefore silver coins or even spoons were placed in the cradle to protect the newborn baby. A small *sølje* for the child's christening dress was also considered to be insurance against evil supernatural forces.

Mari Sandelien (1873-1962) with a girl's headdress and costume from Valdres. Picture taken before 1893. Contributed by Bjørn Sandelien.

Mari and Engebret Sahl from Hallingdal, probable wedding picture from 1894; grandparents of Mary Fry. Contributed by Bjørn Sandelien.

Each bunad today usually has its own silver jewelry, sometimes based on old copies, other times silver newly created for a special bunad or festdrakt. The advice from the Norwegian Bunad and Folk Dress Board is that for all bunads copies of old costume silver from the same district as the bunad may be used. It is not advisable to wear traditional silver from a different area. There is, however, available some costume silver which is not for any specific region, and which may be used with any bunad. If you are lucky enough to have any old inherited jewelry, you may use that as well.

Until the early 1800's all jewelry was produced in the cities, where gold and silversmiths by law had to reside.

Earrings and bracelets are not part of the traditional folk costumes. Earrings based on the design of the costume's silver are nevertheless popular today. Silver buckles on the shoes and finger rings of silver were quite common in the old days. Buttons, clasps and hooks could be made from silver, pewter or brass. In many places, and among ordinary people, very little jewelry was used. Sometimes a small pin *(sølje)*, used to keep the shirt closed at the neck, would have to do.

Bridal silver, of course, was in a class by itself. Most of the old silver belts belonged to a bridal outfit. It was, together with much of the other bridal silver, something most people either borrowed

Neck button from Kari Gjerde's family, Voss 1830's and six gilt, old støler from Thorbjørn Gjerde's family (Hardanger). Contributed by Kari and Thørbjörn Gjerde.

A very old traditional piece of jewelry used in some areas by married women, or in particular, brides, is the agnsti or Agnus Dei

or rented. Today some bunads have silver belts, adopted from the old folk costumes, and in addition quite elaborate and expensive jewelry. A very old traditional piece of jewelry used in some areas by married women, and in particular brides, is the agnsti or *Agnus Dei*. It could be a locket or a large silver coin worn on a chain, and often decorated with engravings of religious symbols, in addition to attachments. Some have filigree decorations as well. The origin of this piece of jewelry is to be found in the Middle Ages. The locket could, for instance, contain money for an offering in the church, or perhaps smelling salts.

If you are a lucky owner of a bunad, you don't have to wear the most expensive and elaborate jewelry. This is something which can be acquired over time - which was the way it mostly used to be in the old days.

As we can see, a bunad today is the result of a very long tradition, with a gradual development over many years. A great deal of work lies behind the finished product. It is important to know a little bit about this tradition and its development so we may treat this rich heritage with respect. A bunad can last for many years and will never become unfashionable. That is if you do not change it according to recent fashion by, for example, altering the length of the skirt or the placement of the waistline. When you maintain the fashion of the period the bunad hailed from, you are not subject to changes in style, and therefore have a costume which is correct at all times.

Gilt Agnus Dei on a flat silver chain, at least 150 years old. Contributed by Hulda Velken.

CHAPTER II

The Bunad Tradition in Southern California

TOP OF PAGE:
Belt worn by a married woman, Hardanger ca. 50 years old. Contributed by Hulda Velken.

IN THE AREA OF Southern California which has been researched, a variety of different costumes are represented. The 108 festive bunads that have been registered come from all over Norway. Except for one province *(fylke)*, Aust-Agder, all others are represented, with the most from Hordaland. Hardanger is the district of Hordaland that in particular is well represented, with eighteen complete or almost complete costumes. This is not very surprising since the Hardanger bunad for a long time was very popular, and used in many parts of Norway as a "national costume." Only nine or ten of these costumes are owned by people with direct family connections to Hardanger. Some of these bunads are very old as well—100 years old or more. Other popular costumes in our district include: Nordland (5), Sunnmøre (7), Voss (6), Hallingdal (6), Valdres (6), Rondastakks (11) and Oslo (5).

The information on the questionnaire used to gather the necessary data for this publication shows that most bunad owners either by inheritance or their own choice have bunads from the districts their families came from or are otherwise strongly connected to by marriage. There are, however, some who have chosen a festdrakt or bunad without any family ties to the district where it originated. This is often done because the costume appealed to the individual, or the owner's Norwegian ancestors are so far removed in time that no particular feeling of belonging to any district in Norway has survived. Nevertheless, it has been surprising and encouraging to see how many of the recent acquisitions are rooted in a genuine desire to have an authentic and traditional costume representing the owner's family heritage. Over the past two years about fifteen new bunads have been acquired in the district. That is more than a thirteen percent increase over a short period. This reflects that the strong interest for bunads in Norway has also had a positive effect in Southern California. One fact must be mentioned. Regrettably there are few men with bunads in Southern California. It is hoped that

the new bunad enthusiasm among men in Norway will rub off on Norwegian-American males as well. As men in Norway already have found out, men in Southern California may also realize that women are charmed by men in striking costumes, that is to say men in bunads!

In this chapter, each type of bunad will be discussed, beginning in the north of Norway and moving south. After the general description of the costume, the different participants in the project will be mentioned, with brief information about their bunad and family background.

Finnmark

The Kautokeino Sami Women's Costumes

Today Samis are spread all over Norway. A sizeable number, for instance, live in Oslo. Although most Samis in Norway today wear modern clothing, in the traditional Sami areas of Finnmark quite a few still wear their folk costumes on a regular basis. Their folk costumes have, in other words, an unbroken tradition up to our own time. Within the large area from Femunden (Hedmark province) in the south to Finnmark in the north, where Samis traditionally have lived, there are different Sami costume areas with certain similarities, but also quite a few dissimilarities.

Some of the most colorful and lavishly decorated ones are found in Kautokeino. It is also interesting to see that the cut of the men's costumes *(kofter)* are similar to the women's costumes or *kofter,* except that the women's costumes are longer and quite a bit wider. Although *kofte* was commonly used by men in Norway in the Middle Ages and in some places up to the 19th century, the Sami kofte has had its own separate tradition for many hundred years. Over time changes occurred, but the basics have remained. Today there are quite a variety of choices in dress material, colors, and decorations for women. Overall it can be said that the closer a bunad or costume is to a living folk costume tradition, the more variety there is in fabrics and details. Sami children wear smaller versions of the grown-up costumes.

The Kautokeino woman's costume may be made of wool, cotton or silk fabric. It is most often sewn from blue wool fabric, but may also be in red, green, yellow or white. It is decorated with strips of cloth, ribbons and cords in contrasting colors. The colors are composed according to tradition, but an individual style also is important. By seeing the decorative pattern, an expert can very often identify the seamstress. Wide sections or borders of decorations are attached to the sleeves and the hem of

Kautokeino Sami bunads: *Beryle Young, Annika Schaffroth and Greta Berg* *(See pages 38-39).*

the skirt. The one on the skirt may be creased or pleated. The length of the *kofte* and the width of the decorated border may vary a great deal.

The cap is made of red wool and decorated with ribbons and rick-rack trimmings in contrasting colors. The top of the cap is made of a round piece of fabric, gathered and fastened to a wide band, which surrounds the head. Earflaps are attached to this part. They have ribbons attached to tie the cap under the chin. The colors of the cap decorations vary a great deal, depending on the seamstress and local tradition.

A square shawl folded in a triangle and often with handmade fringes is placed around the neck and fastened by a silver or gilt *sølje.* The pin may also be made of reindeer horn. The Kautokeino women often wear many large pins, either in silver or gilt silver. The shawl may be in many different colors. A white damask weave shawl is often used for weddings and other important occasions. The belts are based on old Sami patterns and are tablet woven. The main color is white, with red, green and blue patterns. The belt may also be of leather covered with silver or gilt buttons. Married women wear square buttons, girls round ones.

In the winter *bellinger* and *skaller* are used. *Bellinger* are leggings made of reindeer skin. A strip of red cloth is fastened to them. *Skaller* are shoes of reindeer skin with the fur still on and with a curved-up tip in front. Traditionally they were filled with a special type of straw *(sennegras)* for cushioning. The shoes are fastened around the ankles with woven ribbons in several colors, different for men and women. In the summer *komager* are used. They are basically the same as *skaller,* but made of cowhide. Today you will often see more modern footwear with the costumes. White mittens with red, green and blue patterns are used on the many cold days. A large woolen shawl is also added for warmth.

Kari Berg

Kari was born in Trondheim, Norway. Her family moved to the United States in 1950, and settled in San Diego. However, Kari went back to Norway and lived there, first in 1964-65, and later she and her husband and daughter lived in Norway for fourteen years, and of these nine years in Kautokeino. While in Kautokeino, she became very interested in weaving. She even won a prize for a *grene*, a traditional Sami woven rug. Kari acquired a Sami costume from Kautokeino when she lived there. It was purchased around 1982 and was new at the time. Greta Berg is posing in her sister's costume. *(See photo, page 37)*

Kirsten Hawkins Brune

Kirsten is the daughter of Kari Berg and is Greta Berg's niece. As a teenager, Kirsten lived with her parents in Kautokeino. Her father was a

Kautokeino Sami bunads: *Kirsten Hawkins Brune and Solfrid Hætta. Photo courtesy of National Geographic* *(See pages 38-39).*

math and science teacher at the local high school. In addition, he was an avid dog sled driver (musher). Today mushing is a tourist attraction in Karasjok, another Sami town. Kirsten went to the local primary and secondary schools in Kautokeino, where she made her own summer *kofte* as a project. This was in 1983 when she was 14. In February 1983 she and a friend, Solfrid Hætta, were pictured in their Sami costumes in National Geographic Magazine in an article about "Peoples of the Arctic." Kirsten was wearing her summer *kofte* in this photograph, and Solfrid was wearing a winter costume with a pair of roller skates, borrowed from Kirsten. It is quite a picture. In addition to her summer costume, Kirsten was also given a beautiful winter, or year round, *kofte* for her confirmation. Her costume is complete, with all parts worn with the outfit. Beryle Young is posing in Kirsten's winter costume, and Annika Schaffroth is wearing the summer costume. *(See photo, page 37)*

Nordland and Troms

The Nordland Bunad

For many years this costume represented all of northern Norway, but today there are quite a few other bunads and festdrakts representing the three northernmost provinces of Norway. The Nordland bunad is inspired primarily by old pieces of clothing from the Vefsen area of Nordland province. For this reason it is also called the Vefsen bunad. The style is copied from a silk dress with no embroidery, which was in common use during the 19th century. The skirt has deep soft pleats in front and is tightly shirred *(piperynka)* in the back. At the time of the bunad's reconstruction in the 1920's, it was considered more Norwegian, and hence more desirable, to use Norwegian produced fabrics and wool embroidery. The costume is therefore made of green or blue woolen broadcloth or woolen tabby and embroidered. The embroidery on the skirt, bodice, and purse was copied from an old pattern found at Røyten in Nordland. The pattern was taken from a purse and a bodice insert. The largest and dominant flower of the embroidery is a red water lily. This costume was completed and presented to the public in 1928.

The white linen shirt for the costume has white embroidery, based on the same embroidery pattern as the rest of the dress. The apron and shawl are of checked blue or green hand-woven or commercial (factory made) mercerized cotton. A cap *(rynkehue)* is made of either blue or green mercerized cotton with no embroidery, but with a narrow lace trim in front. It is based on an old black church cap that once was in common use. A cape of wool brocade, either in green or blue, lined in yellow wool and with a silver clasp for closing, is also a part of this outfit. White or black stockings should be used, as well as black bunad shoes with silver buckles.

Goldsmith Rørvik in Mosjøen designed the jewelry for this costume. The purse clasp, cuff links and clasps on the bodice and cape are engraved with a water lily. A large pin, or *sølje,* with silver or gold attachments, and a smaller one in silver with oxidized or gilt silver attachments, are part of the jewelry for this bunad.

Anne Kløvnes Høidal *(See photo next page)*

Anne was born and raised on Uløy in Troms. In the coastal area where she came from, the bunad tradition was not very strong. Most women who had a bunad used the Nordland bunad, since at the time no separate costume for Troms had been worked out. One of Anne's great-

Nordland bunads: *Anne Kløvnes Høidal, Thelma Johannesen, Marit Knaplund Folts (See pages 40 and 42).*

grandmothers came from the Sandnessjøen area in Nordland. Her family had lived there for three hundred years, so the Nordland connection was pretty strong. One of her aunts had a bunad from Nordland, and her sister Elsa attended a folk high school in Trondarnes, which was a promoter of the folk costume and bunad tradition. Her sister made her own bunad while studying there, and was a great help when Anne assembled her own bunad in 1985. Most of the consultation was done by long distance phone calls. Anne's costume is green. In addition to her bunad silver for her Nordland costume, she has a collection of Sami silver pins. An old larger Telemark *sølje* was added to the collection when she was lucky enough to come across the pin at a thrift shop in La Mesa while looking for a Halloween costume for her son. Anne came to San Diego in 1967, where her husband, Oddvar, has taught courses in Scandinavian and Modern European history for many years at San Diego State University. She and her family have kept in close contact with Norway by extended visits.

Thelma J. Johannesen *(See photo, page 41)*

Thelma made her bunad in October 1994. Since she has excellent sewing skills, she did the embroidery and assembled the costume herself. She also completed the shawl and apron, which arrived unfinished from Norway. Thelma's bunad is green.

Thelma is married to a Norwegian-American, Allen Johannesen, a past President of House of Norway. Allen's father, who was a sailor in the Norwegian merchant marine, came from Tromsø. Thelma performs as a singer both in choirs and as a soloist. She and her husband have long been active in the Norwegian-American community, and Thelma felt her bunad would be put to good use. She is often called upon to perform at major events, where her costume fits right in.

Marit Knaplund Folts *(See photo, page 41)*

Marit is truly a "*nordlandsjente*" (a girl from Nordland). She was born at Saltstraumen near Bodø in Nordland province. For her it was natural to have a Nordland bunad. Her niece, who also embroidered it, gave the green costume to her. Her two sisters in Norway and many other relatives have the same Nordland bunad as Marit. As Marit herself says, "In Norway it is natural to choose a bunad from the area you come from."

Grete Anne Hemmingsen Porteous

During one of her family's many visits to Norway, Grete's father, Edvard Hemmingsen, who is a *tromsøgutt* (a boy from Tromsø), decided to give his daughter a bunad that reflected his heritage in northern Norway.

***Nordland bunads:** Wendy Hovland-Henry and Mary Peterson DeNino (See pages 42 and 44).*

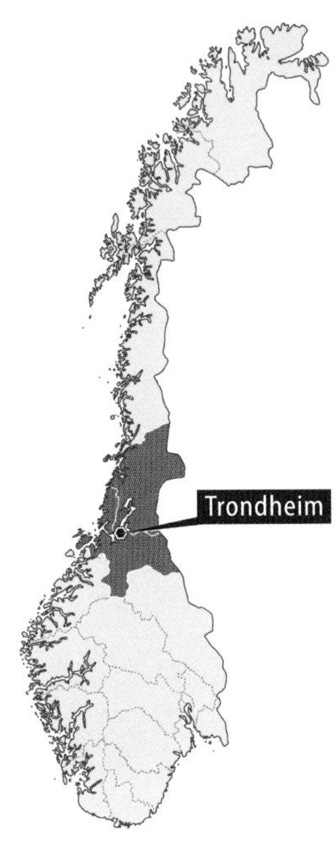

Her blue bunad was made to order by Husfliden in Tromsø. When the costume arrived in San Diego, her parents wanted to take some pictures of her in the new bunad, and they went to La Jolla Cove. A Korean tourist suddenly jumped out of his car. He became very enthusiastic and snapped many pictures. Unfortunately, due to language difficulties, he did not understand that this was a Norwegian national costume; so somewhere in Korea her costume is probably labeled a California costume. Wendy Hovland-Henry is posing in Grete's costume. *(See photo, page 43)*

Mary Peterson De Nino *(See photo, page 43)*

Mary's father was born in Lenvik, a small fishing village in Troms. Her great grandfather had quite a reputation locally as a fisherman. He was also stubborn. Unfortunately, he refused to throw out his hard-won catch during a severe storm, and, as a result, drowned when the boat capsized. His son, however, was rescued. His experience may have been a factor in Mary's grand-father's decision to try homesteading in western North Dakota. Mary's father was three years old when he arrived in the United States.

Mary has visited Norway twice. The first time was with her husband, John, who decided that she should have a beautiful blue bunad from Nordland. Mary keeps in touch with her Norwegian roots through correspondence or by visiting relatives.

Trøndelag

The Namdalen Bunad

The idea of a separate festive bunad for Namdalen surfaced first in 1923, but the final result did not appear before the 1950's. The prototypes for the bunad and its silver were found in Paul Woxeng's collection at Vikna. An old green wool skirt with a black printed pattern was copied. The color was named *gjæslinggrønn* because seaweed used for the green coloring came from the fishing port of Gjæslingan. The pattern is hand printed. Old original wood printing blocks from Sverresborg Museum were copied for this purpose. The skirt is pleated and has a red border at the bottom.

The vest is made of a bright red silk damask weave with flaps in front and deep pleats in the back. It is closed by two silver clasps and a concealed hook at the top. The original for the vest came from Overhalla. The black velvet cap with wide silk ribbons for tying it under the chin came from Nordli. A large scarf is also part of the costume.

Trøndelag Namdalen bunad: *Agnes Sprækenhus Meum* *(See next page).*

Each woman is supposed to use her favorite scarf, which provides for an individual touch. The shirt is of white linen, with embroidery in white on both collar and cuffs.

The stockings for the costume are most often made of fine wool in the same color as the vest. The bunad shoes have silver buckles of a local pattern. The dress silver is patterned after old pewter jewelry from the Woxeng collection and consists of clasps for the vest, cuff links, a small pin for the shirt, and a large pin *(bringesølje)*. The purse is composed of the same red silk damask as the vest and has a black velvet insert. The purse clasp is made of brass.

Agnes Spräkenhus Meum *(See photo, page 45)*

Both of Agnes' parents were born in Ytre Namdal. Agnes came to the United States in 1963, and when she married in 1968, she acquired her bunad for the wedding. "Since I was going to be living in the U.S.A., I especially wanted a bunad. My aunt was thrilled to provide any information I needed." Naturally, Agnes chose a *namdalsbunad* because that is the one used in her district of Norway. Her aunt was the official distributor of this costume. Her aunt made the costume for her, with the help of Agnes' two sisters in Norway. Both Agnes' sister and sister-in-law have the same bunad, as do quite a few other relatives. Some of her nieces have been given a bunad for their confirmation. It was an old tradition to give a young woman's costume to a girl for her confirmation. This custom has become very popular again.

The Nord-Trøndelag Bunad

The North Trøndelag bunad was reconstructed and finished in 1938. There are three color variations for this bunad: blue, wine red and rusty red, all made of fine wool. The two red variations have basically the same embroidery pattern; the blue has a different one. Like most other bunads from Trøndelag, these show the Rococo influence both in cut and choice of materials. The blue costume is very much based on an old wedding dress from 1753, originally from Inderøy. The wool embroidery pattern is composed of seven colors, depicting the tree of life branching out. The blue costume has its own shirt, a copy of one found at Sverresborg Museum.

The red costumes are embroidered with white linen thread. The wine red one also has some appliqués. The skirt for all costumes is softly pleated. Based on surviving examples of historic clothing, we know that in the latter half of the 18th century damask woven fabrics were very popular in Trøndelag. The vest for the rusty red and blue costumes is made of hand woven damask linen of the same shade as the

Nord-Trøndelag bunad: *Greta Berg (See page 48).*

skirt. The wine red costume has a golden silk damask vest. All vests have a Rococo shape with flaps in front and back. Two silver clasps and a pin at the top close the vest.

An embroidered silk cap with a lace border in front is used with all three costumes. The purse is made of the same fabric and color as the bunad, but has a leather back part. The embroidery on the purse reflects the border on the skirt. There is a short cape, also of the same fabric as the bunad, or a black jacket of the same cut as the vest may be used. Black traditional bunad shoes are worn with white stockings.

In the 18th century silk scarves were often purchased at market places like the one at Levanger. At the time some of the scarves very likely came from Sweden. The connection between Trøndelag and Sweden was close at times. Today a hand woven silk scarf is used, in matching colors with the costume.

Silver jewelry for the North Trøndelag bunad consists of a small round pin with hanging filigree and disk attachments to close the shirt in front, and a large round pin, also with attachments, which is fastened at the top of the vest. The large pin also holds the scarf in place. The vest is held together by two silver clasps at the waist. Silver cuff links, shoe buckles and a purse clasp, either in silver or bronze with silver overlay, complete the jewelry for this costume.

Greta Berg *(See photo, page 47)*

Greta has strong family ties to Trøndelag. Her father, Kai Berg, grew up there after his family moved from Gøteborg, Sweden, when he was a year old. Greta's mother, Judith Thevik, was born in Selbu, and Greta's older sister, Kari, was born in Trondheim. However, Greta's maternal grandmother, Anna Olivia Lonmo, came from Namsos in North Trøndelag. When Greta saw the blue bunad from North Trøndelag, this was the one she selected for herself.

Greta bought her bunad kit in 1977. She lived in Tromsø at the time, where she studied on a Rotary International Foundation Fellowship. Her mother and aunt in California did the embroidery for her. The costume was then sent back to Norway to be assembled by experts.

Greta's family emigrated from Norway to California in 1950. Greta and her brother Carl were born in San Diego. As Kai and Judith needed to learn English, they did not speak Norwegian to Greta and Carl. However, Greta learned the language when she was a student in Norway. She has kept up her skills and speaks Norwegian fluently. Quite an accomplishment!

The Trønder Bunad

When this bunad was reconstructed in 1920-23, it was meant to be a costume for the entire province. However, since 1923 several additional bunads have emerged. Today this Trønder bunad is mainly worn in South Trøndelag. At the time of its reconstruction, no folk costumes were still in use in Trøndelag except at Røros. Nevertheless, it was possible to collect many different pieces of costumes, and some pictures showed what the old folk costumes had looked like. It became evident that the Rococo fashion of the 18th century had been popular in much of Trøndelag. This style was therefore chosen.

Both the vest and skirt of the Trønder bunad are in matching colors, either in blue, green or rusty red. Many of the old vests which were registered were of fine imported fabrics. However, in the 1920's the dominant trend was to use Norwegian fabrics. The vest of the Trønder bunad is in wool damask, woven with linen warp. It is in the same color as the skirt, but the linen warp is in gray, giving it a two-colored look. It has flaps in front and a gathered back edged in red, or a green edging on the red vest. Two silver clasps and a hook close the vest in front. The skirt is in a matching solid color to the vest. In the old days striped fabrics were also used. A gray and white linen apron in damask weave is used for all three colors of the bunad.

The shirt is of white linen, today mostly with crewel white-on-white embroidery. Counted thread embroidery is also used. There is a choice between a silk cap with a many colored rose pattern embroidery, and a head square in linen with drawn work. The model for this particular head square came from Selbu. It was originally used by a bride on her way to church. Often a bridal head square was later used to wrap the newborn child being christened. The square is mounted over a red role padding.

The purse for the Trønder bunad is of black wool with a floral wool embroidery. The back piece may be of leather, and the clasp and hook are made of silver or brass. Stockings are red, except for the red costume, which has green stockings. Shoes are traditional black bunad shoes with silver buckles. The outerwear is a cape of blue or green wool damask.

The silver jewelry for the Trønder bunad includes a collar pin, a *sølje* with hanging leaves and cuff links. An *Agnus Dei* pendant is also often used.

Dale Guernsey Roybal *(See photo, page 51)*

During the summer of 1988 when Dale visited her relatives in Trøndelag, she bought the materials to make a bunad. A cousin of Dale also made a bunad for herself after having been to Norway, and last year Dale's sister, Peggy, brought back a child's costume for her four-year-old granddaughter. The bunad interest in Dale's family is not new. Her grandmother, Serine Heitlo, had a large painted photograph of herself in a Hardanger bunad displayed for many years in the window of the local photographer's store in Verdal. Serine met her husband, who was born in North Dakota, when his family returned to Norway for a brief three-year stay. Since Dale's mother's family has its roots in Trøndelag, it was natural for her to choose a bunad similar to that of her relatives in Norway.

Dale started sewing her costume when she joined Sons of Norway in 2000. She has been working on the bunad at the House of Norway, in Balboa Park, where several ladies who are interested in making their own bunads have met and worked on their costumes. Lizzie Riiber has translated sewing directions for them and provided advice. In the process Dale has become so accomplished that she has sewn a couple of other bunads as well.

Helga Sigrid Eggen Moore *(See photo next page)*

Helga comes from Orkdal in South Trøndelag. She has a Trønder bunad which she acquired in the early 1970's. It was made in Orkdal by a seamstress, who was authorized to make this costume. Helga's costume is blue, and she has the embroidered cap. There are many other members of Helga's family who own bunads, and all of them have a Trønder bunad.

After Helga became active in House of Norway and Sons of Norway in San Diego, she decided to buy a bunad. For her it was rather simple since her next-door neighbor in Norway was a bunad maker. Kaspara Kyllingstad, the neighbor, was one of the original creators of the Trønder bunad. Helga is the proud owner of a *sølje* and a purse clasp which came from her maternal grandmother's family in Numedal. Her paternal grandmother made the *nuppereller*, or tatting, around the collar and cuffs on Helga's bunad shirt.

The Røros Bunad

The Røros bunad is based on a very long unbroken folk costume tradition. It was in daily use up until 1900. Later it became a bunad for festive occasions. Many old folk costumes are preserved in the Røros area, so there is accurate and detailed knowledge about the different types of costumes that were used in this district. For instance, there is still a difference in dress between young unmarried women and married ones. This difference is noticeable especially in the caps as well as the jackets.

***Trønder bunad:** Dale Guernsey Roybal and Helga Sigrid Eggen Moore (See pages 49 and 50).*

TRØNDELAG

The married women *(kjerringer)* always wear a black cap, which is called *ørhue*. It has a black bow in the back, and is also tied under the chin with wide black ribbons. The girls' caps are much more colorful.

There are several color options and patterns for this bunad; for the skirt, apron, and shawl. The *kjerringdrakt,* married woman's bunad, which is shown here, has a black or dark blue wool jacket with a ruffled back flap. It is strongly influenced by the Biedermeier fashion of the 1800's. Notice the puff sleeves. The belted and fitted jacket is called a *spensel.* This jacket is not an outer garment, but part of the dress. A small white scarf is worn at the neck under a large wool or silk shawl, which is either checked or with a flower motif. The softly pleated skirt is either of checked or striped wool of various colors, but red or reddish brown is often the basic colors. The finely pleated apron may be in wool or silk, with a checked or floral pattern, or in a single color. The purse, or pocket, is in a single colored wool fabric, embroidered with a floral pattern, and with a leather backing. The purse clasp and hook are made of brass.

The costume is worn over a wool or cotton underskirt with a ruffle at the bottom. In the old days a quilted underskirt was worn on cold days. In Røros those days were many. A long linen "shirt" or chemise was used as an undergarment. A blue, semi-long, damask cape in silk with a fur collar is still used on cold days. Black traditional shoes with silver buckles and black stockings are worn with this costume today.

Juanita Ballard Griebel *(See photo next page)*

Røros, the old mining town in South Trøndelag, is where Juanita's Norwegian ancestors came from. Her great grandfather and his wife immigrated to Iowa in 1869. The voyage over the Atlantic Ocean lasted much longer than anticipated, so they almost starved to death. Also, the first two years of farming ended in disaster when grasshoppers wiped out their crops. They moved on to Minnesota, where they helped found the Hitterdal community. During the summer of 2000 Juanita visited relatives in Røros and decided to purchase a Røros bunad. She has the so-called *kjerringdrakt,* which, as mentioned earlier, is used by married women. Her costume was made by professionals.

Røros bunad: *Juanita Ballard Griebel (See previous page).*

Møre og Romsdal

The Nordmøre Bunad

The Nordmøre bunad reflects the folk costume tradition of the interior of Nordmøre as it was in the first half of the 19th century. In the early 1920's a reconstruction of this bunad began. There were no complete costumes available for study, but many pieces of clothing from different places in this area provided ample source material. A complete costume was finished in 1939, but unfortunately it was destroyed as a result of a fire in Kristiansund during World War II. A new reconstruction was later made and several variations added. Finally in the late 1970's the present-day costume was finished in co-operation with the Norwegian Bunad and Folk Dress Board.

There are many variations in color and fabrics to chose from for this bunad, which allows for individual ideas and tastes. The skirt is usually in black or blue wool tabby or damask, but may also be in a brown or green color. It is tightly shirred around the waist *(piperynka).* The long apron is either of hand-woven checked cotton and mohair in blue, green, brown, pink or black, or of white linen with double cutwork.

There are also several choices for the bodice *(oppluten).* These include fabrics of a bright red or very dark pink wool damask with bird motifs. Also blue-green wool damask may be chosen, as well as pink glossy wool of satin weave with designs (calamanco). The bodice is edged in front with gold or silver ribbons and closed with concealed hooks. A belt of the same material as the skirt is decorated with silver attachments, or it may be embroidered in many colors. Both belts are closed by a silver clasp.

There are two choices for the white linen shirt. The stand-up collar, cuffs and shoulders may be embroidered with a counted thread embroidery, white-on-white, or traced white work. The Nordmøre area is well known for its beautiful embroideries. The purse may be of the same material and color as the skirt, with different embroidery versions to chose from. The headdress is either a white linen cap with a narrow silk scarf, or a pointed cap *(pikhue)* in black, blue or brown velvet with an embroidered ribbon in front. The color of the cap is often chosen to match the skirt.

The bunad has a blue or black wadmel (homespun) cape or jacket. The jacket is short and edged with a gold or silver ribbon. Today stockings are red or black, and shoes, of course, are the traditional ones. The silver jewelry for this costume is copied from old pieces. There is a particular collar button to close the shirt. It has either long or short attach-

Nordmøre bunad: *Margaret Filius (See page 56).*

ments with dangling leaves. An *Agnus Dei* locket is sometimes used.

Margaret Filius *(See photo, page 55)*

Margaret used to live in Denver, Colorado, where she was a folk dancer in the Boulder Scandia Folk Dance Group. It was a requirement that all dancers have authentic folk costumes. Since Margaret is of Scottish heritage, she felt the west coast of Norway, with old Viking connections to Scotland, would be the best place for her to look for a bunad. She chose the Nordmøre bunad because she had a Norwegian dancer friend who could help her acquire a costume from this area.

Margaret has a very fine costume bought in 1979. She has all the required pieces, except a headdress. Her bunad skirt is black. The black apron has a square pattern in red, brown and green. The vest is red brocade edged with a silver lace. Her purse is black with embroidery. Margaret wears red stockings, and she has bunad shoes. The jewelry for her costume includes an *Agnus Dei* medallion on a chain.

The Ørskog Bunad

The Ørskog bunad is the best-known bunad from the Sunnmøre district. There are, however, many varieties of this costume in this area. They all have the same basic cut, but vary in embroidery patterns and colors. Most of them have enough individual characteristics to be labeled as separate bunads. There are, however, two very similar versions of the Ørskog bunad, separated only by the embroidery pattern on the bodice. The so-called Sunnmøre version uses the same pattern on the bodice as on the apron. The Oslo version, developed by people living in Oslo who originally came from Sunnmøre, has heart shaped roses on the bodice.

The reconstruction of this particular bunad from old folk costume pieces started in earnest in the 1920's. A bunad had already been in limited use, but additional source material was collected, and in 1927 the new version was exhibited in Ålesund. This bunad has also been called the "Märtha bunad" because Crown Princess Märtha was presented with one, and in the 1990's the same bunad was given to Princess Märtha Louise as well.

The bunad is available in black or dark blue woolen broadcloth or tabby. It has a heavily embroidered apron of the same fabric and of the same length as the skirt. The apron is edged in red wool. The costume is embroidered in many colors, mainly in blue, pink, red and white. The embroidery pattern comes from an old bodice and apron found in Ørskog. Characteristic of this embroidery are the small white "drops of light," which are placed at the end of each leaf or next to it. Other characteristic parts of the embroidery are the heart shaped rose, the lily and the tree of life. The skirt is softly pleated or has pressed pleats. It may also be gathered at the waist. An embroidered belt covers the waistline, and a woven band is often used along the hem of the skirt.

The bodice is embroidered both on the front and back. It has a narrow red wool edging, and is closed by concealed hooks. The purse, which is also of the same fabric as the rest of the outfit, is embroidered with part of the same embroidery pattern as the apron. It also has a narrow red edging. The shirt is of white linen with white embroidery. There are three different shirt models to choose from.

Red stockings for girls or black stockings for adult women, plus black bunad shoes, are worn with the costume. A cape is worn as an outer garment. It is semi-long with a stand-up collar and closed by a silver clasp. There is a white linen head-square embroidered in black for married women, and one with red or multi-colored embroidery for girls. A dark, very narrow silk scarf is wound around the head and tied with a bow in front to fasten the square. There is, however, more precedence for a couple of other headdresses in this area. *Høgehuer* (high caps) or *kollehuer* (round caps) were probably much more common in the old days than the scarves. The strikingly embroidered *kollehue* is therefore also an option for young girls today. The cap is made of the same fabric and in the same color as the bunad.

Copies of old dress silver from Sunnmøre are available. The most distinctive piece is perhaps the Sunnmøre collar button with long silver attachments. A round silver pin with attached leaves and small silver knobs is also used on the shirt. The purse clasp is most often of brass, but may also be of silver.

Randi Sjaastad Pogue *(See photo, page 59)*

Randi grew up on Ellingsøy, an island near Ålesund. To attend high school, she had to use a ferry to go to Ålesund. She emigrated in 1983. Today she lives in Rancho Bernardo with her husband and two children.

Randi's mother, Liv, decided that both her daughters should have a bunad from Sunnmøre. In 1974 a friend of her mother's finished Randi's bunad, which is the Ørskog bunad. Randi's children had Norwegian costumes when they were quite young. Since they have outgrown these, she is thinking of acquiring new ones. Randi is presently the treasurer of the San Diego chapter of the Norse Federation. She is also a member of the House of Norway.

Aud Listhaug McKernan *(No photo)*

Aud actually comes from Ørskog in Sunnmøre. She emigrated in 1968.

In 1962 she had acquired a kit for an Ørskog bunad. It was purchased at Heimen in Oslo, but was embroidered by an old lady in Ørskog. Aud's mother, sister and sister-in-law as well as nieces in Norway all have the same costume. This bunad was chosen because it represents Aud's district of Norway and she thought it to be a beautiful costume for festive occasions. Aud spends her summers in Norway, where she has a summer home.

Girls' Costumes from Sunnmøre

Adeline Svendsen *(See photo next page)*

Adeline has a bunad from 1926. It started out as a girl's costume. Since the official Ørskog bunad, which this costume resembles, was presented in 1927, hers must be one of the first costumes of this kind which was made for girls. At the time when she obtained her outfit, Roald Amundsen was scheduled to visit Spokane, Washington, where she lived. It was going to be "a whistle stop. The Sons of Norway Lodge (Tordenskjold # 5) rallied around the idea of a celebration and decided that flowers should be presented, and I was the lucky little girl who got to do it." A bunad was needed in a hurry, and a kit was sent from relatives in Norway. Her mother made the bunad. After the exciting visit, the bodice was sent back to Norway to be reworked. Adeline was twelve when she was given this costume. It has been enlarged over the years, and Adeline still wears it with pride. There are many in Adeline's family in Norway who own a Sunnmøre bunad.

Kimberly Hanken Bardin

Kimberly is the owner of a girl's costume from Sunnmøre. It was given to her by her paternal grandmother, Gertrude Hanken, in ca. 1970. Her grandfather, Carl Hanken, came from the small island of Hanken near Ålesund. Mr. Hanken was a commercial tuna fisherman with his own boat after he settled in San Diego. Both Gertrude and Carl were very active in Valhall Lodge, Sons of Norway. Carl was President of the Lodge, and both of them participated in many activities in the Norwegian-American community. Kimberly can remember taking part in lodge festivities with her grandparents as a girl. "I spent countless hours helping them with their activities. I began attending 17th of May celebrations in 1972 with my grandparents, and I never missed a celebration for nearly 20 years. We looked forward to this outing and I treasure those memories dearly. Grandma loved to tell everyone each year that I still was wearing the same costume [I had received as a little girl]". Kimberly attended the flag raising ceremony on May 17 in Balboa Park

Sunnmøre bunads: *Randi Sjaastad Pogue (See page 57), Adeline Svendsen (See page 58) and Lizzie Skyllstad Riiber (See page 60).*

with her grandmother as long as she lived.

Heather, Kimberly's daughter, is posing in her mother's costume. According to Husfliden in Ålesund, this bunad was designed sometime in the 1920' or 1930's. The date is a bit uncertain. The costume is used over a wide area of Sunnmøre, but the embroidery design is based on the Nordal and the Ørskog patterns. This embroidery has not been altered over the years and is used only on girls' costumes.

(See photo next page)

The Hjørundfjord Bunad

Lizzie Skyllstad Riiber *(See photo, page 59)*

Lizzie comes from a family with a very rich bunad tradition. Many members of her family have bunads, representing several districts like Sunnmøre, Valdres, Hallingdal and Gudbrandsdalen. When she was five, she inherited a Hallingdal bunad from her mother. This costume was originally made for her mother by her grandmother. The fabric (wadmel) came from a suit which her great-grandfather, born in 1848, had used.

Dressed up in her heavy and itchy costume, Lizzie and her family traveled from Oslo to Eidsvoll to celebrate May 17. Their Opel was decorated with birch branches and flags, and the whole family was decorated with 17th of May *sløyfer* (ribbons). It was a fantastic experience for a five-year-old girl to be part of the 17th of May celebration at this place, where Norwegian independence was proclaimed in 1814. "The intense feeling of being in the middle of something unique was overwhelming. I experience this feeling even today every time I put on my bunad. It makes me feel so proud."

Today Lizzie owns three bunads, one of them a Hjørundfjord bunad from Sunnmøre, which is similar to the Ørskog bunad in cut and color, but has a different embroidery pattern, although much the same colors. Lizzie also has a white head square with black embroidery, a *koneskaut,* a married woman's headdress. Lizzie chose a Sunnmøre costume because her father came from Skyllstad in Nordangdalen. Lizzie purchased her bunad from Husfliden in Ålesund in 1951. Since there is an old folk costume tradition in Lizzie's family, she owns several parts of old costumes, like embroidered suspenders, a cap in silk damask, another headpiece in lace and an old purse.

***Sunnmøre bunads:** Kimberly Hanken Bardin with daughter Heather* *(See pages 58, 60, 62).*

MØRE OG ROMSDAL

The Nordal / Sykkylven Bunad

Aprell Waymire

Aprell inherited her bunad from her grandmother, Borghild Andersen, in 1995. Borghild was born and raised in Ålesund. Aprell thinks her grandmother herself may have made this costume. Borghild immigrated to the United States in 1927 and eventually settled in San Diego, where her husband, Aslak K. (A. K.) Andersen was a commercial fisherman.

The exact district Aprell's bunad comes from has been somewhat difficult to pinpoint. After consulting with Husfliden in Ålesund, we know they do not sell it, nor do they know exactly where in the Sunnmøre district it comes from. However, it reminds one most of the Nordal bunad, as well as a bit of the Sykkylven costume. Sunnmøre Museum in Ålesund could not identify this particular costume either. It is, however, very clear that this bunad comes from Sunnmøre.

The costume consists of a fitted bodice and attached softly pleated skirt in black wool. The bodice is edged in red velvet and embroidered in front and on the back. The main embroidery colors are yellow, red and light blue. There is also a narrow embroidered belt. The main motif on the front of the bodice is a version of the typical Sunnmøre *hjerterose* (heart shaped rose). The apron has the equally typical Sunnmøre "drops of light" at the end of the leaves, as well as a twisting embroidered border on the apron, also frequently seen on costumes from Sunnmøre. Kimberly Hanken Bardin is posing in Aprell's bunad. *(See photo, page 61)*

The Ørsta Bunad

This bunad is not the most common bunad in Sunnmøre, although it seems to be gaining in popularity. It was finished in 1947. Aslaug Hagen did the drawing of the embroidery pattern, and the painter Karl Straume provided some advice. The bunad is based on old local textiles and embroidery patterns.

The skirt, bodice, purse and cap are either in black or dark blue wool. The skirt has nine repetitions of a floral pattern along the bottom. It is softly pleated. The same floral pattern we find on the skirt is modified and used on the bodice, purse and cap. This bunad does not have an apron.

The bodice has a deep cut front. It often has a narrow red edging, and is closed by clasps. The shirt is of white linen with white hemstitch embroidery on collar, cuffs and along the opening in the front. It is a copy of a shirt from the 1850's.

Ørsta bunad: *Sonja Valderhaug Howard* *(See page 64).*

The purse has a brass clasp and hook made after an old one from the Engeset farm. The well-known woodcarver Lars Kinsarvik made the mold for the reconstructed clasp, which is hand cast also today. The bunad silver consists of an Ørsta button to close the shirt. It has two long hanging attachments. Cuff links are in the same pattern. A round pin with attached leaves is added to the finery.

The cap is an embroidered *kollehue* based on an 1850's design. This cap is especially used among the young. A white linen head square may also be used with this costume. A long cape, called a church coat or cape, is used as an outer garment. Stockings are red for girls, but black for adults. The shoes have silver buckles.

Sonja Valderhaug Howard *(See photo, page 63)*

Sonja's mother, Eldbjørg Valderhaug, who came from the Ørsta district, gave Sonja her Ørsta bunad. Eldbjørg herself received the costume in 1945 as a gift from her mother and brother, Nils, who had hired a professional seamstress, Nanna Myklebust, to make the costume.

According to Eldbjørg, this bunad has an embroidery pattern based on the embroidery found on an old purse used by her mother, Synnøve Kolås. Synnøve had inherited this purse from her grandmother, Anne Helena Bjørdal. According to Eldbjørg, Sonja's cousin, Anna Marie Øyehaug, who lives in Ørsta, Sunnmøre, now owns the original purse. Many of Eldbjørg's and Sonja's relatives in Norway have Sunnmøre costumes. Sonja also has some old silver jewelry, up to 100 years old.

Sogn og Fjordane

The Sunnfjord Bunad

Information and old costumes were collected already in 1914 for the study and reconstruction of this bunad. The Sunnfjord bunad was based on solid source material and finished in 1922. Reconstruction was based on old garments and on what people still remembered about old folk costumes. The bunad has a bodice of green wool fabric, edged with tablet woven braids. A decorative cross-stitched band with pewter eyelets and a chain close the bodice. The same woven pattern found on the edging of the bodice is repeated in the belt, which has two long streamers in front.

The skirt of this costume is made of black woolen tabby or broadcloth and has wide pressed pleats, except for a section in front, which is flat. The bottom of the skirt is edged in green. Two woven braids of the

Sunnfjord bunad: *Brit Backous Montalbano (See page 66).*

same type as on the bodice circle the skirt above the green edging. A woven diagonally striped apron of mercerized cotton is optional.

The shirt is of coarse linen, with several choices of white embroidery. One of these is patterned after an old shirt from Florø. It has broad borders of drawn work on the front, collar and cuffs. A small dark cap with a lace edge in front is available as a headdress. A couple of different purses can be worn with this outfit. One is green like the bodice, rather square and decorated with cross-stitch embroidery. The purse clasp and hook are in brass and are hung from the waistband on the left side under the apron. Black bunad shoes and black stockings are recommended. Earlier pewter jewelry was quite common in this bunad district. Today oxidized silver has become popular. The jewelry is copied from old pieces made in Bergen in the 1700's and 1800's.

Mary Josoy Stedham

Many years ago Mary was given the bunad of her mother, Amanda Josoy. Amanda's maiden name was Brendehaug. In 1958 she came to San Diego from Fjaler in Sunnfjord. Part of this bunad was made by Amanda herself; the rest was purchased in Norway. The costume is 50-60 years old, so it is the older version of the Sunnfjord bunad, not the one that was revised in 1987.

Mary has not seen her mother wear an apron or purse with the costume. Amanda used a blouse with a crocheted collar and cuffs. As a teenager, Mary wore this bunad when she danced with the Rolling Trolls, a folk dance group in San Diego. Brit Backous Montalbano is posing in Mary's costume. *(See photo, page 65)*

HORDALAND

Nordhordland Festbunad

The North Hordaland Festive Bunad for Women

North Hordaland has a long unbroken folk costume and bunad tradition for women. Between 1900-1950 the festive bunad in this area was strongly influenced by the Hardanger bunad. This trend has later been reversed. The Bunad and Folk Costume Board recommended the reconstructed North Hordaland festive bunad in 1992. Today there are three bunads to choose from in this area: the festive one, the black winter bunad and the green jacket bunad *(grønntrøyebunad).*

The bodice of the festive bunad is in red wool cloth, edged with yellow and green woven silk ribbons *(krokakvarde).* The skirt is either black

Nordhordland Festbunad: *Eldbjørg Tveit Backous (See next page).*

or dark blue, most often in wool. It may be pleated with narrow pleats or gathered at the waist. At the hem there may be a colored woven ribbon or a velvet one.

The shirt is in white linen, and may have different white or black embroidery. The most commonly used pattern has openwork embroidery. The apron is in white linen, most often with openwork embroidery as well. Girls wear a woven wreath around the head. Women have a white cap-like headdress *(kvithue)* with a role padding. A variety of bodice inserts exist in North Hordaland, and many of the older ones are copied today. Girls wear a pearl or wool embroidered belt, married women often wear a belt with silver ornaments.

The dress silver is gilt and consists of a collar button, a pin *(sølje)* and cuff links. Sometimes round ornaments *(borer)* are attached to the bodice in front.

Black stockings and black bunad shoes are worn. A blue or black wool jacket with seven-inch long flaps is used as an outer garment.

Eldbjørg Tveit Backous *(See photo, page 67)*

Eldbjørg's home place was Holsnøy, Meland County, in North Hordaland. She grew up on the Tveit farm, but started to travel early. As a young girl, she went to England as an au pair to learn the language. A few years later (1960) she had a chance to come to the United States, where she married and settled.

Eldbjørg has her mother's bunad, which her father won at a raffle and gave to her mother around 1960. Members of Frekhaug Husmorlag (Frekhaug Homemakers Association) made the costume. Her outfit is quite similar to the above description, except that Eldbjørg has a wool embroidered belt (cross-stitched) and a crocheted insert on her apron.

Eldbjørg also has most of the parts for two girls' Hardanger bunads, which were given to her by Hardanger relatives. Her daughter, Brit, used a Hardanger costume as a girl.

The Hardanger Bunad

Hordaland province is undoubtedly the area with the greatest variety of bunads in Norway. The festive folk costumes from Hardanger, Voss, Fana and some other places never went out of use. For most of the other costume areas in the province there was also much source material to support the reconstructions of today's bunads. The Hardanger costume was the first Norwegian folk costume to win broad popularity outside of its own district. It became so popular that it was adopted as a "national costume" for all of Norway. This period started at the end of the nineteenth century and lasted for more than fifty years. For that reason we find many old pieces of this costume all over Norway, as well as in the United States. Although the old folk costumes for festive occasions never went out of use in Hardanger, over the years some changes took place. The costume we today call the Hardanger bunad comes from Sørfjorden, but even within this district there are quite a few variations of the costume. A wealth of different embroidery patterns exists for the apron and shirt. The same variety is found in the bodice inserts, belts and broad streamers hanging down from the married woman's silver belt. All of these can be woven or embroidered in different techniques. At an exhibit of bodice inserts from Hordaland (1700-1990) in 1996 over 1000 different inserts were shown. Today the insert for the Hardanger bunad is most often embroidered with pearls.

The skirt *(stakk)* of the dress is made from black or dark blue woolen tabby or wadmel. It may be decorated with black silk or velvet ribbons at the bottom. Deep pleats are used in some areas; in others the skirt is shirred at the waist. The fitted bodice *(uppluten)* may be of red or green wool or brocade, edged by woven rose-patterned ribbons and closed by concealed hooks. Previously there was far more variation in the choice of fabric, such as velvet, silk damask and several types of wool. The bodice has a broad insert which, as mentioned, may be decorated in many ways.

The white linen or cotton shirt has either white Hardanger (openwork) embroidery or black embroidery on cuffs, collar and front. It is shirred at the neck. The long apron may be made of white linen or cotton with Hardanger embroidery.

A belt with gilt silver ornaments is part of a married woman's outfit. Girls wear embroidered belts. A central streamer *(fanglenja),* decorated with silver ornaments, accompanies the silver belt. Two additional streamers *(breidaband)*, either embroidered or woven, are also attached to the belt. Only married women wear starched white narrowly pleated head squares with role padding. Unfortunately this headdress is very difficult to arrange, resulting in both married and unmarried women wearing the headband or wreath. A small pearl embroidered cap is also frequently used. Black stockings and black bunad shoes are worn, and the outer garment is a black cape, lined in red.

The dress silver consists of a collar button with hanging attachments, cuff links and a *sølje.* Married women wear a belt with silver attachments, as already mentioned. Married women may also wear an *Agnus Dei,* a large medallion or coin on a broad, flat silver chain. All the silver for this costume is usually gilded, except the cuff links, the collar button, and the chain for the *Agnus Dei.*

Hordaland

Hanne Berg *(See photo next page)*

Hanne comes from a family with several Hardanger bunads. Although Hanne grew up in Oslo, she ended up with a Hardanger bunad. Her mother's family came from Hardanger, and as children both Hanne and her sisters had costumes from this area. As adults, both her sisters in Norway have this costume, and in 2000 Hanne inherited her bunad from an aunt in Norway. The bunad is 35-40 years old and was made by her aunt, who made numerous costumes and did other fine handiwork. Hanne has also inherited several exquisite tablecloths embroidered by the same aunt.

Hanne's bunad is very complete. She owns a small pearl embroidered cap as well as a pear shaped purse with pearl embroidery and a pewter clasp and hook. The silver which belongs to the bunad was hand-made. Hanne's father comes from Telemark, and as a young person Hanne frequently visited a silversmith at Notodden, where she helped make *søljer.* It must have been a very interesting experience.

Hulda Langesæter Velken *(See photo next page)*

Hulda grew up on a very steep fruit-producing farm in Kinsarvik in Sørfjorden. There was a very strong folk costume tradition in this community. It was common for girls to receive their first grown-up bunad for their confirmation at age 14 or 15, which is what Hulda experienced. Hulda's mother embroidered and made her apron and blouse. The apron is an exceptionally fine example of Hardanger embroidery. Hulda still has the old garments, including the black pleated skirt of 68 years and a very beautiful red velvet bodice with a beaded insert. She also has a red wool bodice as well as a bodice insert of a more recent date.

Hulda has some very interesting old bunad silver, some of which definitely appears to be handmade. Her large gilt filigree decorated *Agnus Dei* pendant, with red and green stones and many attachments, is probably around 150 years old. *(See page 34)* It is a stunningly beautiful piece of jewelry. She also has a gilt silver belt with cross motifs on each attachment, in addition to a woven belt and streamers, which at first glance look embroidered. Her cuff links came from her mother, who gave all her children similar sets of cuff links.

Bianca Paige Einemo *(See photo, page 87)*

Bianca is the daughter of Trond Einemo, who was born in Øystese in Hardanger. Bianca has always been fascinated with bunads. She has been lucky to be able to visit Norway every year, and most members of her family in Hardanger own bunads. One time Bianca borrowed a

Hardanger bunads: *Hanne Berg and Hulda LangesæterVelken (See previous page).*

bunad from her cousin in Norway to wear for May 17 in San Diego. When Bianca became Junior Princess of the House of Norway in Balboa Park, it seemed a good time for her to acquire a Hardanger bunad.

Bianca is very proud of her Norwegian background and looks forward to showing her heritage as part of House of Norway. She is also fortunate to have a bunad which consists of both new and old pieces. Bianca received her outfit in April 2001. The bunad was made in Voss by Ragnhild Skjoldli. Lizzie Riiber did the fitting in San Diego, and Bianca's grandmother, Gyda Einemo, did some finishing touches while on a visit from Norway. The bodice insert was given to Bianca by her grandmother, Gyda, who in turn had inherited it from her grandmother, Brita Fykse. It dates back to the 1800's. Bianca's grandmother also wore the pearl embroidered belt when she was young. Trond's brothers-in-law provided the jewelry for Bianca's bunad. They are both goldsmiths and have stores in Geilo and Ål in Hallingdal. They also produce handmade jewelry.

Mary Otto Fry

Mary's Hardanger bunad was inherited from her mother, Birgit Sahl Otto (1894-1983), who brought it with her when she immigrated to the United States in 1920. Birgit was born in Ål, Hallingdal, but was confirmed in Oslo in 1909. She did all the beadwork and embroidery for the costume herself when confirmed. Quite an accomplishment at that age. She wore a *sølje* with a red stone which belonged to her mother, Mari Sandelien. It was later passed on to Birgit, Mari's oldest daughter. Birgit later gave Mary, her oldest daughter, this *sølje*. It has been said that "silver pieces which were handed down carry family spirits, and for that reason become spiritually more valuable." Today Birgit's bunad is very fragile, but still treasured as a family heirloom. *(See page 19)*

Linda Annin Pettersen *(See photo next page)*

Not long ago Linda was the lucky recipient of an approximately 70-year-old Hardanger bunad. The original owner had passed away, and her friends with whom she was living gave it to Linda. The costume is complete with a small hat. Linda is married to Alf Pettersen, a Norwegian-American. Both Linda and Alf are very active members of Norge Lodge 60 in Vista, where Alf has served as President and Linda as Treasurer. Linda wears her costume for lodge functions and other events in the Norwegian-American community. She also owns a Rogaland everyday costume which she has made herself.

Hardanger bunads: *Linda Annin Pettersen, Eva Quale Strum and Janet Kurz Weber* *(See pages 72 and 74).*

Hordaland

Eva Quale Strum *(See photo, page 73)*

Eva immigrated to Seattle from Trondheim in 1929. When she was 8 years old her mother picked out a Hardanger bunad for her. Eva still wears the beaded bodice insert of the old costume, but she bought the rest of her present bunad from a store in Tacoma, Washington, which imported bunad fabrics from Norway and had the costumes made locally. A 92-year-old lady in Tacoma made the embroidery on her apron and shirt. Eva does not know if any other family members own a bunad.

Jeanette Olsen Kurz

"It started in about 1955 when my sister, Rakel, was at a flea market in Bay Ridge, Brooklyn, New York and spotted a Hardanger bodice insert. No one else knew what it was, but she purchased it for $2.00. My sister framed it, and it hung in the vestibule of our parents' home for many years." This, according to Jeanette, is the beginning of her bunad.

When Jeanette turned 40, her sister offered to make her a complete bunad. A 90-year-old Norwegian lady made the embroidered insert for the apron. Rakel made the vest and skirt. Jeanette made the shirt herself and added an antique Hardanger embroidered collar and cuffs. She also made the belt trimmed with beads. Jeanette's husband, Bob, bought her first *sølje* for their 10th wedding anniversary, and a second for their 45th.

Jeanette and Bob have been very active in Sons of Norway, first at Long Island, New York, and in later years in San Diego, California, so Jeanette has used her bunad quite often. These days their daughter, Janet Weber, enjoys wearing her costume on May 17th for the House of Norway parade in Balboa Park in San Diego. Janet is posing in her mother's costume. *(See photo, page 73)*

Marit Olson Vincent *(See photo next page)*

Marit's Hardanger bunad is the result of the work of three generations of women in her family. The vest and bodice insert were purchased in Norway, but the apron and the beaded belt were made by her grandmother, Clara Negaard. Marit's aunt, Jean Shogren, made the skirt. Marit made the beautiful Hardanger embroidery on the collar and cuffs of her blouse.

The traditon of owning and wearing a Hardanger costume goes back to Marit's grandmother. Her mother, Rosalie Olson, and aunt, Jean Shogren, also own this costume. They are posing together with Marit in the picture in this book.

Hardanger bunads: *Marit Olson Vincent, Rosalie Negaard Olson and Jean Negaard Shogren* *(See pages 74 and 76).*

Hordaland

Rosalie Negaard Olson *(See photo, page 75)*

All four of Rosalie's grandparents came from Norway in the late 1860's and early 1870's. Rosalie has been to Norway several times. In addition to a Lundeby costume, Rosalie also owns a Hardanger bunad. Her mother, Clara Negaard, similarly had a Hardanger costume, and in 1975 she gave one to Rosalie. Her mother embroidered the apron and made the beaded belt. She purchased the bodice insert from Norway and sewed the vest using braids from Norway. Rosalie's sister, Jean Shogren, sewed the skirt. The Hardanger collar and cuffs were made by Myrtle Whitworth, a long-time friend and fellow Sons of Norway member.

Jean Negaard Shogren *(See photo, page 75)*

Jean's Norwegian ancestors came from Hedmark, Sigdal, and Land in the 1860's. She has a solid bunad tradition in her family. There are several Hardanger bunads and Lillehammer, or Lundeby, costumes in her family. Jean sewed the vest for her Hardanger bunad after a pattern her mother, Clara Negaard, bought from Norway. Her mother made the beaded belt and purchased the beaded bodice insert from Norway. Esther Dyer, a friend and fellow member of Valhall Lodge in San Diego, gave Jean the embroidered insert for the apron, which Jean finished herself. The Hardanger embroidered collar and cuffs for the shirt were a recent gift from Myrtle Whitworth, a longtime member of Valhall Lodge. Jean sewed the shirt after a pattern provided by Myrtle. The beaded cap was made by Jean's mother to match the bodice insert.

Myrtle Hovland Whitworth *(See photo next page)*

Both of Myrtle's parents came from Norway. Her father, Jacob Jacobson Hovland, emigrated from Hovland in Sørfjorden, a long side arm of the Hardanger Fjord, and her mother, Disa Jordal Årtun, came from Odda, also in the Hardanger Fjord. Her father came to the United States in 1903 with his family, and her mother arrived in 1910, while the rest of her mother's family came in 1922.

There is a very long bunad tradition in Myrtle's family. She owns a costume which was used by her mother's mother, born in 1863, and parts of another, which belonged to her mother. Her mother, Disa, who was born in 1894, received her bunad for her confirmation.

In 1935 Myrtle was given mother Disa's costume so she could wear it for the World Exposition in Balboa Park in San Diego. Old embroidered cuffs and a collar were also inherited and later used on a blouse for one of Myrtle's granddaughters. Myrtle herself has done quite a bit of Hardanger embroidery, and she has made the costumes for her great-

Four generations in Hardanger bunads: *Front: Myrtle Whitworth, Amanda and Jennifer Saunders. Back: Jane Whitworth and Annelle Saunders (See pages 76 and 78). Photo courtesy of Expressly Portraits, Sondra Cleveland.*

granddaughters. She owns many old parts of Hardanger costumes. Among her treasures are two sharply creased *(pliserte)* head squares, an old girl's cap, several aprons, blouses, bodices and inserts, all very lovingly taken care of.

Annelle Jane Saunders, Amanda Jeanette and Jennifer Samantha Saunders *(See photo, page 77)*

Annelle is the daughter of Jane Whitworth and granddaughter of Myrtle Hovland Whitworth. She comes from an old Hardanger family with quite a bunad tradition. Annelle's daughters, Amanda (8) and Jennifer (3), have costumes which great-grandmother Myrtle has made. Parts of the costumes are old. For instance, Amanda has cuffs and the collar on her bunad shirt which were part of a child's shirt for Myrtle's aunt Jenny, who passed away in the 1920's.

Jane Ann Whitworth *(See photo, page 77)*

Jane has visited Norway several times. After a trip to Hardanger in 1986 to visit her mother's relatives, she was fortunate to receive from different relatives many of the handmade parts of a Hardanger bunad. Her mother, Myrtle Whitworth, put all the pieces together for her. This is a very special outfit for Jane since so many family members and friends worked together to give her this beautiful bunad. She is collecting the gilt silver attachments necessary to put a belt together at a later date.

The bunad tradition in the Whitworth family is alive and very well. As mentioned above, both of Jane's daughters and her four granddaughters have Hardanger bunads. Great-grandmother Myrtle Whitworth has made the girls' bunads, which are proudly worn for festive occasions.

Olaug Nilsen Lelevier

Olaug owns a girl's Hardanger bunad that was given to her 30 years ago. It was a gift from a cousin in Flekkefjord, whose daughter had outgrown the costume. Olaug's cousin, Sissel Skoland, had embroidered the apron and shirt, but the beaded pieces were bought. When the family lived in Arizona, Olaug's daughter, Rhoda, wore the costume for Norwegian celebrations. Two of Olaug's granddaughters, Chanel and Destiny Rose, have later worn the bunad. Destiny Rose Sheehan is posing in the bunad for the picture in this book. *(See photo next page and on page 95)*

Eldbjørg Backous and Lorraine Tucker *(No photos)*

Eldbjørg Backous has almost two complete Hardanger bunads for girls ages 8-10. Eldbjørg's daughter used the costumes when she was a girl.

Hardanger bunads: *Destiny Rose Sheehan and Annalisa Hawkinson Ritchie* *(See pages 78 and 79).*

Lorraine Tucker inherited parts of a Hardanger bunad from her mother, Emma Reinholdtsen, who came from Nordfjord. It was considered to be a national costume at the time she acquired her bunad, and therefore used by people all over Norway.

Lizzie Riiber

Annalisa Hawkinson Ritchie is the granddaughter of Tamara and Sigurd Stautland. She is posing in a girl's Hardanger bunad owned by Lizzie Riiber. The costume, including a beautiful beaded belt and a bodice insert, was made by Ragnhild Skjoldli from Voss who is known for her fine beadwork. The cap Annalisa is wearing is an antique pearl embroidered cap belonging to House of Norway in Balboa Park. The jewelry was borrowed from Annalisa's grandmother, Tamara Stautland. *(See photo above)*

The Voss Bunad for Women

In Voss the old folk costume tradition has been very strong, and the women's festive outfits have changed relatively little since the 1850's. The folk costumes in this district have continued to be used up to our own time, with some changes taking place. In particular, there used to be more variations in the shirt, apron, belt and bodice insert. However, the existing variety is still considerable, allowing for quite a bit of individual taste and style. The women's costumes have maintained several distinctions between a married woman and a girl. Only married women have the "right" to wear a silver belt and a broad silver chain.

The skirt *(dossa)* of this bunad is of dark blue wool with a very broad green edge at the bottom. It has deep loose pleats with a flat section in front. A silver lace covers the transition on the skirt between the blue and green. Girls have no green border, but three black velvet ribbons instead. The bodice of red wool has a broad (4 cm.) green edging and a ribbon of stringed pearls where the bodice and edging come together. In the back the bodice is cut very wide around the arms. The bodice is shorter than the natural waistline. A red wool insert with pearl embroidery and a black velvet top edge is used in the deeply cut front opening of the bodice. Many patterns for the pearl embroidery exist, but the most common today is the one with an eight-petal rose in the center.

The long apron is of white linen or cotton with white openwork embroidery. The white shirt, which may be in linen or cotton, is embroidered in black *(svartsaumsbroderi)* for married women; girls have white embroidery on their shirt. The white starched linen head square for married women is also embroidered in black. It is arranged over a role padding.

Married women wear a red belt with attached silver ornaments and a silver clasp. Girls use a pearl embroidered belt with a silver clasp. The dress silver consists of a collar button with two long attachments and often decorated with two red stones, a round pin *(sølje)* with attachments, and cuff links. Married women also wear a flat broad silver chain, often with a *"dalar"* (a large coin) as a pendant. The *"dalar"* is fastened at the top of the bodice insert with a hook. All jewelry, except the chain and cuff links, are gold plated.

Black stockings and bunad shoes are worn with this costume. The outer garment can either be a black cape or a large checked shawl.

Kari Songve Gjerde *(See photo next page)*

Kari was born and raised in Voss. She was given her first costume for her confirmation in 1940. At the time she made her own embroidered belt. The bodice insert, however, was inherited from her grandmother. The shirt and apron were borrowed from her sister. This was during World War II, when fabric was hard to come by. Later she made her own shirt, and an elderly expert made her apron, using the pattern from her grandmother's apron.

When Kari married, she was given a silver belt, which had been in her husband's family since 1837-38. She also has a pair of old pins

Voss bunads: *Kari Songve Gjerde, Kristin Gjerde and Mattias Henning (See pages 80, 82 and 84).*

(søljer) from her grandmother. They also date back to the 1830's. Some very old round button-like attachments, *(støler),* which were used along the opening on the bodice of bridal outfits, are from the Gjerde family. Kari has several old costume pieces, like bodice inserts and vests.

All women, and some men, in Kari's family own a bunad. In Norway she can count 28 close relatives with a Voss bunad. In this country her daughters, Kristin and Nora, have Voss costumes and a four-year-old grandson, Mattias Henning, also has one. Kari is a very accomplished and recognized rosemaler.

Kristin Gjerde *(See photo, page 81)*

Kristin is the daughter of Torbjørn and Kari Gjerde from Voss. She was given her bunad when she was 15 or 16 years old, at the age when most girls in Voss are confirmed and acquire their first young woman's bunad. Parts of Kristin's costume were passed down to her from her mother and other relatives. Her mother, who is an expert seamstress, also made some parts for her. As a teenager, Kristin was a member of the Rolling Trolls folk dance group where she always wore her bunad.

Nora Gjerde Stark *(See photo next page)*

Nora is also a daughter of Torbjørn and Kari Gjerde. Her costume is naturally a Voss bunad, composed of parts from different relatives. "I got bits and pieces from my grandmother and several aunts. My mother also provided some parts." Nora's mother assembled everything and finished the bunad. It is part of Nora's family tradition to have a bunad from Voss. Her bunad is a tangible example of how history and the tradition of several generations of one family can blend and merge in one single costume.

Bergljot (Bell) Belsnes Lirhus *(See photo, page 85)*

Bergljot was the first member of her family to settle in the United States. She came from Voss in 1959. In Norway "every woman in the family" had a bunad, so it was natural for Bergljot to receive a costume for her confirmation.

The present costume which Bergljot wears consists of quite a few older parts which her mother-in-law, Guro Kyte, gave her. The shirt, vest and bodice insert, and in addition the belt, came from Guro. Most people in Bergljot's family have Voss bunads, but a few Hardanger costumes also exist. As a matter of fact, Bergljot inherited a Hardanger costume from her aunt when she passed away. This bunad also consists of some older parts which her aunt had inherited. In addition, Bergljot has inherited some old bunad silver.

Voss bunad: *Nora Gjerde Stark (See previous page).*

HORDALAND

The Voss Bunad for Men

Before 1850 most jackets and vests in Voss were long and the pants were knee breeches. After 1850-1860 a short jacket *(rundtrøya)* and vest were mostly combined with long pants. However, by about 1900 there were very few men who still used the old folk costumes, so when interest in reviving the old costumes emerged in about 1920, research had to be done to establish a costume for men. The one which is in use today resembles very much the folk costume that was worn at the end of the nineteenth century. There is a separate bunad for boys, with knee breeches and a single buttoned red vest. The knee breeches are closed by silver buckles below the knees and are decorated with silver buttons. Both the long pants and the knee breeches have front flaps, closed by buttons. Most men wear long pants today, but knee breeches are also available.

The jacket is made of black wadmel or wool broadcloth. It has a stand-up collar with stitching and turndown lapels. It is double breasted with two rows of seven silver buttons. The jacket is worn open to show off the vest, which is in red cloth with green edging on the stand-up collar. In front the vest has a green panel with red edging made to look as if two vests are worn, which often was the case in the old days. The green "vest" has a double row of buttons and buttonholes. The red vest has two pockets with flaps, edged in green, and the back is made of unbleached linen.

The shirt may be made of linen or cotton with white embroidery on collar and cuffs. White knitted stockings decorated with multi-colored pleated garters are used with the knee breeches. Black bunad shoes with buckles are standard use. A black felt hat is the common headgear for men.

The bunad silver consists of a collar button with attachment, cuff links, silver buttons for the jacket, pants and vest. In addition, a watch chain in silver and a sheath knife may be added.

Mattias Henning *(See photo, page 81)*

Mattias is four years old and the lucky owner of a Voss boy's bunad. He is the son of Kristin Gjerde. Mattias is the third generation of the Gjerde family in Solana Beach with a Voss bunad. His bunad was made by Aslaug Songve, his mother's aunt in Voss.

House of Norway, Balboa Park, San Diego

The House of Norway as an organization has been in operation since April 1935. Its cottage is part of the House of Pacific Relations, which includes 30 national groups represented by 18 cottages in Balboa Park.

Voss bunad: *Bergljot (Bell) Belsnes Lirhus (See page 82).*

Hordaland

The House of Norway was founded as one of the original cottages representing many different nations that were part of the 1935-36 California International Exposition. The international village in the park makes up the House of Pacific Relations, sponsored by the San Diego City Parks and Recreation Department. The House of Norway is an independent, volunteer operated museum and cultural center. The unique cottage features Norwegian culture and heritage and is open to the public every Sunday. Hosts and hostesses provide refreshments and information about Norway and Norwegian culture for those who visit the House of Norway. Thousands of guests from all over the world visit the cottage each year.

The House of Norway offers a unique opportunity for visitors and newcomers to the city to get in touch with Norwegian culture through its many outreach events. It represents "the face of Norway" to all visitors, and as such is of invaluable service to the entire Norwegian-American community in the San Diego area.

Among its many valuable artifacts and possessions, the House of Norway owns a Voss man's bunad and a donated Hardanger fiddle. The story behind the acqusition of the bunad is quite interesting and unique. In 1983 the Edvard Grieg Memorial Foundation of America was established in San Diego as a non-profit organization to promote the memory of Edvard Grieg, his works, and his contributions to the field of music. The officers were Consul Oswald Gilbertson, Chairman, Gary Rundquist, Secretary, and Paul Severtson, Treasurer.

The Grieg Memorial Foundation was very successful in soliciting funds, which were forwarded to the Norwegian Grieg Foundation in Bergen. Funds from this foundation were used in the building of the Troldsalen concert hall at Troldhaugen, Edvard Grieg's home near Bergen, which is now a museum. Because of all the support the Edvard Grieg Memorial Foundation was able to give, its officers were invited to the opening of Troldsalen. The opening took place on May 23, 1985, the centennial of Troldhaugen, a day after the opening of the annual Grieg Festival in Bergen. However, only one member from San Diego was able to participate. He was Paul Severtson, a fine musician and a very capable Hardanger fiddle player. Mr. Severtson had been invited to play at a reception after the opening concert at Troldsalen. House of Norway purchased a Voss bunad for the occasion, which Mr. Severtson proudly wore while he played on the Hardanger fiddle for a selected group of dignitaries, including His Majesty, King Olav V. Today the Voss costume is one of the important possessions of the cottage in addition to the Hardanger fiddle.

Trond Einemo, a member of House of Norway, is posing in the cos-

Hardanger and Voss bunads: *Trond Einemo with daughter Bianca (See pages 70, 84 and 86).*

tume together with his daughter, Bianca, in her Hardanger costume. Bianca is a Junior Princess for the House of Norway in 2001.
(See photo, page 87)

The Bergen Festdrakt

Like most cities, Bergen does not have its own folk costume tradition, although Fana, close by, has one of the oldest living folk costume traditions in Norway. When the city of Oslo created its festdrakt, or festive attire, based on some bunad traditions, Bergen, being a longtime rival, also decided to have one of its own. The first attempt did not succeed, but in 1956 Haldis Nygård created a festive attire based on the outlines of the first attempt.

The Bergen festdrakt comes either in black, dark blue or winter white wool. It has a fitted, embroidered bodice, closed in front by eyelets and a long silver chain. The softly pleated skirt is also embroidered. The same embroidery pattern is seen on the large fringed shawl, small cap and purse. The simple, stylized embroidery is based on traditional Norwegian floral paintings found on furniture and as embroidery patterns. A white cotton poplin blouse with tatting is part of the outfit. Stockings that are the same color as the costume should be used, and the white costume should have white shoes. Black shoes are worn with the dark costumes.

A Bergen jeweler, Egil Monsen, used the design from the 1870's by another jeweler, Theodor Olsen, in creating jewelry designed for this costume. It consists of a large *sølje,* eyelets and a chain for the bodice, a belt (optional) with silver attachments, cuff links and a purse clasp. As a city, Bergen has had many famous gold and silversmiths dating all the way back to the Middle Ages.

Ann Stokke Hougen

Ann has the white Bergen costume, which is less common than the black or dark blue ones. She purchased the kit for this bunad in 1977 when she visited Bergen. Ann did both the embroidery and sewing of the costume. Over the years Ann has been a prolific bunad and costume maker. Not only has she made her sister's Rogaland bunad, and several for herself, but she has also supplied the material for many bunads and even made quite a few of them for other people. Judy Anthonsen is posing in Ann's costume. *(See photo next page)*

Esther Kristoffersen Dyer *(See photo next page)*

Esther comes from the Bergen area in Norway. She has strong family ties to the farm Fanavoll in Fana, outside of Bergen. As a young girl, she

Bergen Festdrakt: *Judy Anthonsen, Esther Dyer and Lorraine Reinholdtsen Tucker (See pages 88 and 89).*

had a Fana bunad, a costume that has an unbroken tradition linking it to the old folk costumes in that district.

Esther arrived in New York with her mother, three brothers and one sister in 1929. They became members of Fram Lodge #11, Sons of Norway, in New York. After Gene, Esther's husband, passed away in 1977, she came to San Diego because she had a sister in Poway. When Esther arrived in San Diego, she became a member of Valhall Lodge #25, Sons of Norway, and a very active member of House of Norway, where she has served with great dedication. On a trip to Bergen on May 17, 1980, Esther decided to acquire a blue bunad representing Bergen. She bought a kit and made the costume herself. Many of her Norwegian relatives have bunads from Fana, Voss and Sogn.

Susan Hansen Luburic *(See photo, page 89 and next page)*

Susan acquired her Bergen costume through eBay on the Internet in July 2000. Her mother, Lorraine Tucker, owns parts of a Hardanger bunad and some older dress silver. These older parts came from Susan's grandmother, Emma Reinholdtsen. Since Emma's family did not come from Hardanger, she acquired her bunad as a "national costume," which was very often done in earlier times.

Susan is the insurance representative for Zone 6, District 6, of Sons of Norway, so she will have a chance to wear her costume often when she visits the different lodges on major occasions. Susan's own Norwegian family roots are in Nordland, Nordfjord, and the Bergen area. Susan's mother, Lorraine Tucker, is modeling with Judy Anthonsen and Esther Dyer in Bergen costumes. Posing in the picture with their mother, Susan, are Mark and Max Luburic in their brand new boys' costumes.

Rogaland

The Rogaland Festive Bunads

There are several festive costumes from Rogaland. The first was researched in 1917, when most folk costumes already were out of use in the district. Stavanger Museum, however, had a collection of folk costumes, and many parts of costumes were still intact in the district. The first costume was reconstructed without much embroidery. For instance, no apron with embroidery was found. However, under the influence of Hulda Garborg, as well as by popular demand, embroidery was used on the cap, purse, shawl and apron. There are many old embroi-

Bergen Festdrakt: *Susan Hansen-Luburic with sons Max and Mark Luburic (seated) (See previous page).*

dery patterns in use.

Most of the festive bunads in this area are made of black wool or wool damask. Some are available also in dark blue or green. The cut of all bunads follow the same basic pattern, based on what was used in the 1850's. The skirt is loosely pleated and attached to the bodice. The apron, also of wool or wool damask, is heavily embroidered, as is the purse and cap. The fitted bodice is of silk damask, single color or with a multi colored pattern, often edged and decorated in the back and front with velvet or silver ribbons. It is closed by a silver chain, drawn through eyelets. The shawl is large and fringed. A short cape is also available as outerwear.

As with most bunads, traditional black shoes are used. Stockings may be black or sometimes red. There is especially designed silver jewelry for some of the costumes. The original jewelry, which the silver for the bunad is copied from, dates back to the 1700's and 1800's.

The Original Old Rogaland Bunad

This Rogaland costume has a black pleated skirt with an apron, and is heavily embroidered. The costume is also available in dark blue. The same embroidery pattern is used for the cap, purse and shawl.

The bodice may be of red or green wool or silk damask, edged with a silver lace. The shirt is in linen with white embroidery *(rogalandsaum).* The cap is based on an old one from 1800 and may be black or red.

Glenda Stokke Holsbo

Glenda comes from a "bunad family." She owns a Rogaland costume, but for a time she also wore her sister's Graffer bunad from Gudbrandsdalen. Her sister, Ann Hougen, owns several bunads and she has made many costumes over the years, among these Glenda's costume. Glenda's parents came from Kristiansund and Hornes in Vest-Agder. They both came from families with a bunad tradition.

Over the years Glenda has been very active in the House of Norway and Sons of Norway. She was president of Sørlandet Lodge in El Cajon, and is presently a member of Valhall Lodge in San Diego. Glenda's friend, Susan Shaddox, is modeling her costume. *(See photo next page)*

Bonita R. Holsbo *(See photo next page)*

Bonita's Norwegian ancestors came from Arendal, Christiania (Oslo) and Trondheim.

The costume Bonita owns was purchased as a kit from Ann Hougen. Bonita embroidered it herself and gave it to her mother, Eva Nelson Holsbo. In 1979 Bonita inherited this bunad from her mother.

Rogaland bunads: *Susan Shaddox and Bonita R. Holsbo (See previous page).*

Bonita's costume has a red silk damask bodice. Bonita wears her costume with pride and in loving memory of her mother.

Olaug Nilsen Lelevier *(See photo next page)*

Olaug hails from Haugesund in Rogaland, and is the proud owner of a Rogaland bunad. As a child she had a Hardanger costume. When she immigrated to the U.S. in 1952, she brought with her another child's size Hardanger bunad.

Olaug's Rogaland costume is a Nordaker costume, an original old Rogaland bunad, made by her mother and aunt with a little outside assistance. Olaug's mother brought it along as a gift when she visited the U.S. in 1977. The skirt, shawl and cap are of fine black wool, heavily embroidered. The bodice is made of light green silk brocade with a multicolored floral pattern. The purse has the same material for its lining as the bodice.

Olaug had always wanted a Rogaland bunad. It has been put to good use since Olaug has been very much involved with the Norse Federation. She was the president for the Phoenix chapter for four years. In San Diego, Olaug is an active member of several Norwegian organizations, including the Norse Federation, where she is the President.

The Jelsa Bunad

Randi Skjæveland Oftedal *(See photo, page 96)*

Randi came to the U.S. from Sandnes in Rogaland in 1959. She acquired her Jelsa Rogaland bunad 15 years ago. She did the embroidery herself, and her mother, who visited from Norway, helped her with the sewing. Randi chose this particular costume for various reasons. She wanted a bunad that was used in her home area in Norway, and she liked the colors of this bunad and the lightweight material. The Jelsa embroidery pattern, based on an old cap, was the first bunad embroidery pattern to be used in Rogaland for a reconstructed costume. Later several other embroidery patterns have followed.

VEST-AGDER

The Vest-Agder Bunad

The bunad is based on old costumes from Vest-Agder province, dating back to 1830-1870. At the beginning of the 20th century, information was gathered from old people who still remembered the costumes well. Old pieces of costumes were also available. In the coastal areas of this prov-

Rogaland and Hardanger bunads: *Olaug Nilsen Lelevier and granddaughter Destiny Rose Sheehan (See pages 78 and 94).*

Rogaland bunad: *Randi Skjæveland Oftedal* *(See page 94).*

ince there was a lively shipping connection with Britain as well as to the continent. As a consequence of trade, fine imported materials were available, which showed up in the costumes.

There are three different types of skirts to choose from for the Vest-Agder bunad. A striped skirt is an option, but the varities in black are the most popular. One black skirt is available with very narrow permanent pleating, while the other is gathered at the waist. There is a red and a green border at the bottom of the skirt. The skirt is held in place by woven suspenders fastened by two silver buttons in front and one in the high cut part of the skirt in the back. This bunad has an underskirt sewn in heavy cotton.

The vest, which is cut high in the middle of the back, is shorter than the natural waistline. It comes in black, red or green wool, or wool damask. It is closed in front by eyelets and a silver chain in addition to a large clasp at the bottom. The white shirt, which can have several types of white embroidery on the collar, cuffs and shoulders, is made of linen or cotton. It has a turndown collar, and the front opening has hemstitch embroidery.

There are three different aprons to choose from for this costume. One is in black wool, embroidered like the shawl; another is in white linen with hemstitch embroidery; and the third is in wool and silk damask, with a green and red pattern.

There is a short wool or wool damask jacket in black for this bunad. The sleeves are wide and creased at the shoulders and taper off toward the wrists. It is cut in the back like the vest, and closed in front with two silver clasps. A large fringed black wool shawl with several embroidery patterns to choose from is widely used. It may either be cut in a square or a triangle. The square shawl is folded in two, often with different colors in the embroidery on each side to signify sorrow or joy. So for a funeral a person would show one side, but for a wedding the other, festive one. The black wool purse has brightly colored wool embroidery, again with several patterns to choose from. The backing of the purse may be of different materials, like wool, leather or burlap. It may be edged in red or green. The clasp and hook for the purse may be of brass or silver. Black or red stockings are worn, and the bunad shoes are black with silver buckles.

The head covering for a married woman is a white linen scarf, embroidered with white hemstitch along the borders. It is fastened over a role padding to make the scarf fall gracefully in the back. Both married and unmarried women may wear a head square, but the role padding for the married women is higher than for the girls. A black wool cap with colorful embroidery is also very popular.

***Vest-Agder bunad:** Magnhild (Malla) Hompland Gilbertson* *(See next page).*

The jewelry for this costume consists of a collar button, cuff links, one or two *søljer;* a small round one below the neck button, then a larger one, heart shaped or round with large disks attached. The silver for the vest and jacket has already been mentioned.

Magnhild (Malla) Hompland Gilbertson *(See photo previous page)*
Malla was born in Kvinesdal, Vest-Agder. She settled in the U.S. in 1958. Malla was given her *festbunad* in 1948/49. As a young girl, she was a member of the Norwegian Youth Association (Noregs Ungdomslag) and took part in a *leikarring,* a folk dance group. This group performed in several parts of Norway.

Malla's pleated black costume was made by her mother, and the silver came from an aunt. Malla is also the owner of a Vest-Agder everyday costume. As the wife of the Norwegian Honorary Consul in San Diego, Oswald Gilbertson, Malla has had ample opportunity to wear her costumes and represent her Norwegian heritage. She has also very graciously let other women borrow her costumes, especially students who have taken part in international festivals and other events.

TELEMARK

The Vest-Telemark Bunad

This bunad is based on a folk costume tradition dating from the 1750's to the beginning of the 19th century. However, several changes have taken place since then, both when the dress was still worn as a folk costume as well as later. Most notably, the waistline has been lowered to one inch above the natural waistline, and the bright floral embroidery on the bodice has been added to the skirt. Today there are quite a few variations of the floral pattern to choose from. The look of the Vest-Telemark bunad was worked out in 1915-1920, and later revised somewhat in the 1950's.

This costume comes with a red or black wool jacket. It is decorated with rose embroidered ribbons, and worn open. The bunad shown in this book has a black wool jacket in the same shape as the red one and with the same embroidery. The gathered skirt, bodice, apron and purse are of black or dark blue woolen tabby. All parts of the costume are embroidered with very bright wool embroidery, with red shades being dominant. The embroidery is called *rosesaum,* or rose work embroidery. It is based on a 150 years old piece of embroidery from the district. The apron, skirt and purse are edged in red, and sometimes in green. There is also a narrow tablet woven belt for the skirt.

The bodice is heavily embroidered both in front and back, trimmed in red and sometimes green as well. It is cut low in the back. In front, a silver chain and eyelets close the bodice. The shirt is in white linen and may have white or multi-colored embroidery on the cuffs and collar. Different headdresses are available. Both married and unmarried women may wear a white linen head square over a role padding. Girls often have a red ribbon with attached silver pieces tied in front of the scarf, and married women have a white lace ribbon instead. A wool scarf or a silk scarf may also be used over the role padding.

Filigree silver is very common in Telemark, which has an unusually rich tradition of bunad silver. There are therefore many choices of dress silver available to choose from in this district. Large gilt pins with raised "beads" and cambers *(boler)* are very popular in this area.

Ann Stokke Hougen

Ann's parents were both born in Norway. Her father came from Kristiansund and her mother from Hornes in Vest-Agder. They immigrated to the United States in 1929. Both her parents were from families with a bunad tradition. One of her grandmothers came from Setesdal and was a folk dancer. Ann's Norwegian husband, Tor, strongly encouraged her in her interest in Norwegian bunads. From her husband's family in Nordmøre, Ann has inherited a very beautiful white embroidered shirt, which is about 200 years old. She is also the lucky owner of an old exceptionally fine *sølje.*

Ann has worked with bunads for many years. She ordered kits from Norway for other people, and very often she did the embroidery and necessary sewing to assemble the costumes. At other times she helped with advice. There are quite a few people in the San Diego area who have acquired their costumes through her. Ann made her own Vest-Telemark bunad, as well as a white Bergen bunad and a Graffer bunad, and a Rogaland bunad for her sister Glenda. *(See pages 89, 93 and 137)*

Perhaps Ann's interest in bunads stems from the fact that when she was a child "I was told I couldn't get a bunad unless I learned to folk dance. As an adult I went into the bunad business, but I never learned to folk dance. Tor (my husband) used to say to my father, it's all your fault, Olav. Luckily they both were laughing." Annika Kovtun is modeling this Telemark costume. *(See photo next page)*

The Aust-Telemark Bunad

There are two main types of costume from the eastern part of Telemark. Perhaps the best known is the one called *"raud-trøye-kleda"*

Vest-Telemark bunad: *Annika Kovtun (See previous page).*

TELEMARK

(the costume with the red jacket). It is based on the festive attire for women, which was used between the latter part of the 18th century and 1850. Queen Sonja, whose ancestors came from Telemark, has this bunad.

Anna Bamble from Heddal started working on a contemporary bunad in about 1920. It was of great concern for her to preserve old sewing techniques and traditional rose embroidery in wool yarn. For instance, she transferred the rose embroidery that had been common on the cloth stockings to the hem of the skirt. However, there is today another East Telemark bunad without any embroidery on the skirt.

The black, green or blue skirt of the East Telemark bunad is in woolen tabby or broadcloth with red, blue and green borders along the hem, or just one border may be used. Anne Bamble's version also has a border of rose embroidery. The skirt is shirred at the waist and has a hidden pocket in one of the side seams. The bodice *(oppluten)* is usually red and covered in front and back by rose embroidery. It is edged with a black rose embroidered border. It is cut to make a wide section of the front open to show the beautiful shirt and showy jewelry. The apron is in the same material as the rest of the costume, with embroidery and most often edged in red. The wide belt for this dress is tablet woven and three inches wide. It sports several colors, but red is the main one.

The jacket is very short, made of red wool with a wide golden border along the bottom. It has rose embroidery in front and back and black borders with embroidery around the wrists. It is closed in front by a concealed hook

The shirt is in white linen or cotton with embroidery in front, on the stand-up collar and the cuffs. There are a great variety of embroidery patterns and colors to choose from. Hardly any two are alike.

There are several headdresses in use for this bunad. A white head square combined with a silk scarf is one option. Another popular head adornment is the *vippe,* a wreath made of woolen tablet woven bands. Black stockings and black traditional shoes should be worn with this costume.

The bodice is adorned with decorative "buttons" *(maljer)* in front. A collar button closes the shirt. One or two large silver pins decorate the shirt in addition to the cuff links. All the silver jewelry for this bunad is based on old traditional patterns. There are a great variety of choices as far as style and execution of the jewelry is concerned, but much of it has filigree decorations, and the size of the pins in particular is quite large.

Aust-Telemark bunad: *Caronne Greenfield Van Nyhuis (See page 104).*

Caronne Greenfield Van Nyhuis *(See photo, page 103)*

"I inherited my bunad from my mother, Clara Hogstad. She was the first in my family to have the privilege to own a bunad." The costume is an East Telemark bunad, made in 1970 by Borgny Tveraaen, who lives in Bamble, Telemark. Borgny is a cousin of Caronne's mother.

Caronne's bunad has both a black skirt and a black bodice. Her skirt has an embroidered border and a green trim. The bodice also has a green trim, and the embroidered apron is trimmed in green as well. Caronne's belt is hand-woven in red, green and gold. The linen shirt for her bunad has black embroidery in front, on the collar and the cuffs. With her bunad, Caronne wears a black wool purse, embroidered on the front and closed by a large filigree clasp. Her bunad jewelry was handmade by a silversmith in Kragerø.

Caronne's Norwegian ancestors came from Jambakkmyra near Sannidal in Telemark (1881) and Inderøy in northern Trøndelag (1866). They immigrated to Remville County, Minnesota. Her mother was quite fluent in Norwegian, and Caronne herself also speaks some Norwegian. Caronne's husband, Steven, has learned quite a bit of Norwegian, so they are both able to converse in Norwegian when they are in Norway.

VESTFOLD

The Vestfold Bunad

The first Vestfold bunad for women was developed in 1932. A living folk costume tradition did not exist in this district at the time, but folk dancing was becoming very popular in the area and many wanted costumes. Quite a bit of research went into the project. It became clear that many different fashions had influenced the way people in this district dressed in the past. The shipping connections to the continent and England had been quite strong for a very long time, and this resulted in many fine and expensive fabrics being used in the past, by men and women who could afford them.

Over the years there have been several revisions of this bunad. In addition to the first, there was one in 1956-58, and the last one was presented in 1993. The version we are showing in this book is the model from 1956-58. All three variations of the bunad have the same basic cut. The later revised costumes have better quality fabrics, and more attention is paid to old sewing techniques. Also, some old parts of costumes that have been found in more recent times were copied and integrated

Vestfold bunad: *Anne Nilsen Engert* *(See next page).*

into the newer costumes.

The black or dark blue skirt of the bunad is softly pleated. The bottom of the skirt is trimmed with a wide border of wadmel in red for the black skirt but green for the blue one. A braid is attached to the upper part of the border. A hand woven trim or ribbon is attached about three inches higher up. The same woven ribbon is used for a belt, which is closed by a silver clasp and buckle. A red cotton underskirt is used with this bunad, with a large pocket and a ruffle at the bottom.

The fitted bodice is either in red or green wadmel with a gray lining of linen. The bodice is trimmed with hand woven braids that match the one on the skirt. It is closed by eyelets and a silver chain. There are two shirts for this costume. One is based on an elaborate bride's shirt, the other, which is more commonly used, is of coarser linen and embroidered in white counted thread work. There are two different kinds of aprons to choose from. One is in white linen with pale floral embroidery. It is copied from an apron from 1820. There is also a woven apron in either blue or dark green wool with contrasting diagonal stripes.

The costume comes with a purse or pocket in the same color and fabric as the skirt. It is most often edged in red. The purse is sometimes embroidered with a floral motif. The purse very often is not used if an apron is worn. Two different caps are available. One model is in pink or black silk damask with a narrow lace trim and ribbons for tying under the chin. A tied bow, in red on the black cap and in black on the pink cap, is fastened in the back. Also used today is another embroidered wool cap, but without ribbons under the chin. The bunad includes a short reversible cape in the same color and fabric as the costume. It is lined in red and closed by a silver clasp.

Red or white stockings are worn with the bunad, and traditional bunad shoes are part of the outfit. The dress jewelry for the Vestfold costume is based on old jewelry which has been found in the district. Most of it is lightly oxidized. In addition to what has already been mentioned, a large round *sølje* with attached disks is commonly used on the shirt. A small round *sølje* keeps the shirt together at the neck, and cuff links close the cuffs.

Anne Nilsen Engert *(See photo, page 105)*

Anne comes from the island of Nøtterø, not far from Tønsberg. People have been seafarers for generations in her district. This included many whalers, and her grandfather was a gunner on a whaling ship. It is therefore not surprising that Anne chose a blue *stakk* or skirt because, as she says, "we lived by the sea." The material for her costume was purchased from Husfliden. Her mother, Wenche Lindaas Nilsen, attended a course on how to make this bunad, and she sewed a Vestfold bunad for both Anne and her sister. Later her mother became gravely ill and although she recovered, she most likely would not have been able to make the costumes. Anne therefore wears her bunad in special appreciation for her mother.

Anne's mother sang in the VAA-RA choir near Tønsberg, whose members were required to wear bunads. Anne thinks this started the bunad tradition in her family. Today her aunts and other members of her family in Norway own bunads. Anne is the only one of her family who lives in the United States. Her costume was given to her for her confirmation in 1985. She wears her costume for Christmas, May 17, christenings and other special occasions.

BUSKERUD

The Southern Buskerud Bunad

The southern part of Buskerud (Nedre Buskerud) does not have the same strong folk costume and bunad tradition as the rest of Buskerud province. A beautiful bunad for the southern or lower part of Buskerud was, however, composed and ready in 1939. The project was spearheaded by Buskerud Bondekvinnelag (a farm women's association), and the well-known architect, Halfdan Arneberg, helped with the reconstruction.

The pleated skirt and bodice of the bunad are made of black or dark green wool. The black underskirt is of lighter material. The fitted bodice is closed in front by silver buttons and a long silver chain. The bodice and hem of the skirt have a very narrow red edging. The wool embroidery on this costume is inspired by decorations on old furniture from Eiker, a part of southern Buskerud. It is kept basically in yellow and gold tones with touches of red and green. There is also a narrow embroidered belt with a silver clasp, as well as a purse and cap with similar embroidery. The cap, now in Drammen Museum, is a copy of an old 18th century cap from Lier.

The shirt similarly is a copy of an old shirt from Fossesholm Manor House. It is sewn in linen and has white embroidery. Old silver from Eiker served as the model for the bunad's dress silver. It consists of a small ring-shaped pin for the shirt; a larger pin fastened below the small one; cuff links, buttons and a chain for the bodice; clasps for the cape, belt and purse; as well as silver buckles for the shoes. Black bunad shoes, black stockings and a cape of the same fabric as the bunad put the finishing touches on this outfit.

Martha Lande Larsen *(See photo next page)*

Martha and her husband Per emigrated from Kongsberg in Buskerud in 1954. They settled in San Diego after a year in Boston. Martha was born Lande and grew up in Kongsberg. When she emigrated, she did not own a bunad, but decided in 1998 to purchase one. Sissel Martinsen, Krokstadelva, who is a professional bunad seamstress, was contacted and in 1999 Per and Martha went to Norway to visit with relatives and to pick up Martha's new costume. They spent May 17th in their old community, and enjoyed seeing all the wonderful bunads in Martha's family. Many of them have the famous "sash costume" *(beltestakk)* from Telemark or East Telemark costumes.

The Sigdal Bunad

In 1938 the Sigdal Association of Farm Women and the Heimen store in Oslo, together with Carsten Lien, started to work on the reconstruction of a bunad from Sigdal. There was a wealth of old costume material in this area. The finished bunad is based on costumes as they were believed to have been in about 1830.

There are many variations of the Sigdal bunad, but the basic cut is the same for all. The skirt is in black or dark blue woolen tabby, tightly shirred except in front, where it has a flat section. It has a very broad embroidered border on the skirt, and is held in place by suspenders. There are four to five different embroidery patterns for the border, based on old preserved borders. The long apron is of the same fabric as the skirt and embroidered with smaller flower motifs than the skirt. It may reach below the main border of the skirt.

The vest for this costume is either of red wool, wool damask or silk damask. It has a gold or silver lace edging in front and along the bottom. An insert with beaded embroidery is attached in the front opening, which is a very wide oval. The insert is optional. The short vest has *skjælinger* in the back. This is an edge reinforced with stiff felt and burlap to make it buckle and stand out a bit.

The jacket, which is in the same fabric as the skirt, also has the same *skjæling* as the vest. It is edged with embroidered borders. A silk scarf around the neck is always worn with the jacket. A fringed black shawl or a lined cape is also available as outer garments. Black stockings and traditional shoes are recommended.

The white linen shirt is shirred at the neck and embroidered in white. A small fully embroidered cap edged in red is the headdress for the Sigdal bunad. It comes in black or dark blue wool. The pocket or

Nedre Buskerud bunad: *Martha Lande Larsen* *(See previous page).*

purse has similar embroidery as the cap.

The silver jewelry for the costume has a long tradition behind it. There have been many accomplished silversmiths in this area for hundreds of years. A collar button or ring-shaped pin closes the shirt. A *sølje* with hanging disks or leaves closes the top of the vest, below which another sølje decorates the front of the shirt. Cuff links and hooks for the jacket, as well as shoe buckles and a purse clasp, complete the jewelry.

Kristin Åby *(See photo next page)*

Kristin's family has long roots in Sigdal. Both her parents were born there, but she grew up in Levanger, North Trøndelag. Kristin's mother has a Sigdal costume, so when Kristin acquired one about twenty years ago, she also chose a Sigdal bunad. An old woman, who worked as a maid for her mother's family, did the embroidery, and a professional seamstress did the sewing. As a matter of fact, Kristin had the border on her skirt copied from an old border found at Hoffart farm, her grandfather's childhood home. The border was found shortly before Kristin got her bunad, so her mother, who has an older Sigdal costume, has a different border on her bunad. Surely this border from her family's farm must make her costume very special to her. Kristin is also the lucky owner of an antique *sølje.* In Kristin's family in Norway there are many bunads, in particular Sigdal bunads and a few Hallingdal bunads.

The Northern Hallingdal Bunad

In the upper *(øvre)* or northern part of Hallingdal, which consists of Ål parish, this bunad has been in continual use from the time it was a folk costume up to our own time. Some changes have occurred over the years, and many variations have gone out of use, but this bunad is an unusually fine traditional costume. Separate headdresses for young girls and married women were used until recently, but today an embroidered cap is generally worn both by young and old. The older *konehette* (wife's cap) is, however, still used by some. It is rather complicated to prepare and mount on the head, which probably explains why it is worn more seldom these days.

The valley of Hallingdal is basically divided in north and south, forming two bunad districts. They have quite a few common traits, but enough individual characteristics and differences to separate the valley into two distinct areas. The bunad from Ål in Hallingdal, like most bunads today, is based on a festive folk costume. The skirt, called *dåsen,* is made of black wool or wool damask, and is tightly gathered and attached to the bodice. The extremely short bodice is of the same fabric. Along the hem of the skirt runs an attached border with very colorful

***Hallingdal and Sigdal bunads:** Kristin Åby and daughter Kjersti Åby Bergquist (See pages 110 and 114).*

Baroque inspired wool embroidery. The same embroidery is repeated on the bodice and cap, although the bodice may be edged in velvet and may have beadwork instead of embroidery. The long apron is often in wool damask with a wide embroidered border at the bottom and a narrower embroidered one at the top, where it is fastened to the bodice.

There are many shirts to choose from in this area, but the most common one is of white cotton with either white or colored embroidery on the collar and cuffs. A small multi-colored scarf may be used around the neck. The outer garment is a short black wool jacket, or a large checkered or printed shawl with fringes may also serve the same purpose. Black traditional shoes with silver buckles and black stockings are part of this outfit.

The jewelry for this Hallingdal bunad is traditional for the area. Notice the two clasps which are fastened on each side of the "suspenders" and connected with three silver chains. In addition, a small round neck pin or *sølje,* a larger *sølje,* and cuff links are used.

Mary Otto Fry *(See photo next page)*

Mary's mother, Birgit Otto (Sahl), was born in 1894 at the Sahl farm in Ål, Hallingdal. She immigrated to the United States (Minneapolis) in 1920 and later married John Otto. Birgit had a Hardanger bunad, which was very popular at the beginning of the 20th century.

Mary has had good contact with her relatives in Norway, both those in Oslo and in Hallingdal. She has family connections to the Sandelien and Sahl farms. When Mary decided to acquire a bunad, she wanted a costume from her mother's home area in Hallingdal. She contacted a second cousin in Oslo who sent her the necessary information. Mary is also the lucky owner of an old *sølje* which belonged to her grandmother. It might even go back further to still another generation.

Bunads from the Southern Part of Hallingdal

Many old costumes are also preserved in the southern parts of the Hallingdal valley. They show a great deal of variety in color, décor, fabric and cut. The folk costumes from Nes, Gol and Hemsedal had a lot in common, and this district formed a separate folk costume area that in some ways was quite distinctive from the Ål costumes. The present-day bunads are based on folk costumes which were in use in the latter part of the 19th century. However, many of their characteristics go back much further in time. Today there are fewer differences than there used to be between the bunads in the north and those in the south of the valley. The women's festive attire in the north and the south originally had different headdresses, aprons and bodices. Today the Gol bunad, for in-

Hallingdal bunads: *Mary Otto Fry and Ellen Groff Holk (See pages 112 and 114).*

stance, has an embroidered cap much like the one in Ål, but you may still see some women wearing a folded silk scarf tied around the head and worn with the cap. The greatest difference between a costume from the north and one from the south is seen in the aprons. In the south the fabric is wool muslin, often printed with a rose pattern on a background of black or blue. Brides traditionally use a white background. Other background colors may be used as well. Checkered wool aprons are also used, often with a rose embroidered border at the bottom. The bodice of the southern costume was always short, but not quite as short as the one for Ål. There are many different embroidery patterns to choose from both for the dress and the shirt. The shirt may be embroidered in white or in a multi-colored pattern.

Kjersti Åby Bergquist *(See photo, page 111)*

Kjersti is 7 years old and the lucky owner of an old Hallingdal bunad. The costume was originally made for her grandmother, probably in 1936, and in time passed on to Kjersti's mother, Kristin Åby. The Hallingdal bunad has over the years been very popular as a children's costume, perhaps because it is so practical for growing girls. Kjersti's bunad has an apron with printed roses and an embroidered small cap with ribbons to be tied under the chin. Perhaps the ribbons were used because without them this small cap would be difficult to keep in place by a small child.

Ellen Groff Holk *(See photo, page 113)*

Both of Ellen's parents came from Norway. Her father, Ole Olsen Groff, emigrated from Finnesgard in Gol, Hallingdal, in about 1888. Her mother also came from Hallingdal, but from Liahagen farm in Torpo. She arrived in the United States in 1900.

Ellen has many relatives in Norway, whom she visits and keeps in close contact with. Many in her mother's family played the Hardanger fiddle. Lora, Ellen's daughter, and Ellen's granddaughter, Rebecca, also play the Hardanger fiddle. They participate every year in workshops for *hardingfele* players. Ellen herself is also very talented musically. She plays the organ and the piano.

Ellen made her own Hallingdal bunad. When working on the embroidery, she demonstrated the technique at a cultural event at Valhall Lodge in San Diego. It took her more than two years to finish her costume. Both Ellen's daughter and granddaughter wear bunads.

In addition to her Hallingdal festive costume, Ellen also owns a blue and white everyday costume from Hallingdal. It was bought at Nesbyen in Hallingdal. Ellen also has made a Rondastakk from Gudbrandsdalen.

Hallingdal bunads: *Lydia Weber and Doris Olsen Cords (See page 116).*

Greta Berg

Lydia Weber is the daughter of Janet Weber, and granddaughter of Jeanette and Bob Kurz of Valhall Lodge, Sons of Norway, in San Diego. She is wearing a Hallingdal costume belonging to her mother's friend, Greta Berg.

Greta found the bunad in 1997 in a Pacific Beach resale shop in San Diego. She immediately recognized it as a Norwegian child's costume and purchased it for $25. It was a lucky find, quite a treasure. The jewelry Lydia is wearing belongs to her mother, Janet. *(See photo, page 115)*

Doris Olsen Cords *(See photo, page 115)*

Doris was born in Kongsberg, Norway. She came to the United States with her parents and her brother in 1927, when she was quite young. Just after arriving from Norway, Doris' mother made her a costume. It was a child's costume that Doris wore with pride for her first May 17 celebration in the United States. Doris has many relatives in Norway. A favorite cousin lives in Gol, Hallingdal. On some occasions, when Doris visited Hallingdal, she borrowed her cousin Randi's Hallingdal bunad. Doris always loved this fine colorful costume. On her 80th birthday in March 2000, her family surprised her with a Hallingdal costume. Under a secret arrangement made by her husband of 59 years, a dear niece and others, some members of her family in Hallingdal did the embroidery and sewing, which took nine months. Other family members gave the silver jewelry. What a wonderful surprise it must have been, especially since Randi and her daughter, with the bunad, showed up for the party in Oceanside, California. Many of Doris' relatives in Norway have different bunads. Doris' oldest daughter has been promised that she will inherit her mother's Hallingdal costume.

OPPLAND

The Vest-Oppland Bunad

No living folk costume tradition existed in this district in the late 1930's when a committee was established to research source material for a costume. A beautiful blue woolen pillow from 1762 was found on one of the large farms in the district. It had originally been used in a sleigh. Both front and back were embroidered with stylized roses and carnations in many colors. A Rococo style bunad was designed in cooperation with Heimen Home Crafts Store in Oslo and architect Halfdan Arneberg, based on the fabric, colors and embroidery of the old pillow.

Vest-Oppland bunad: *Susan Jurasinski Cody (See next page).*

It was introduced in 1939. The cape was added in the 1980's, as was specially designed bunad silver.

The softly pleated skirt of the costume is made of blue woolen tabby or woolen broadcloth. It is embroidered with the pattern from the pillow mentioned above. The vest is of the same fabric, without much embroidery. The shape is based on an old photograph. The vest has four flaps in front, attached to the garment at the waistline. In the back there are no flaps, but a continuation of the back sections with the same length as the front flaps. Around the whole vest there is a narrow embroidered edging in herringbone and French knots. It is closed in front by small eyelets and a silver chain.

The white linen shirt has a shirred neckline and shoulder gussets. It is embroidered in white, probably based on embroidery from an old shawl. The shirt was originally designed in 1926-27 for the Hadeland bunad, another bunad from Vest-Oppland. The shape of old caps from Hadeland inspired the bunad cap. It is embroidered with the design from the front of the old sleigh pillow and edged with the same embroidery as the vest. The purse has the same part of the central embroidery as the cap. A short cape, in the same fabric as the costume and lined with red, is used as outerwear. White or black stockings are worn, along with traditional bunad shoes with buckles.

In 1980 the Vestoppland Home Craft Association started to register the old dress silver in the district. In consultation with Head Curator Aagot Noss at the Norwegian Folk Museum, a selection was made based on this material. The bunad silver consists of a small round pin to close the shirt at the neck, and two other pins or *søljer,* one larger than the other, but both heart shaped and with attachments. As already mentioned, there are a chain and eyelets for closing the vest. There is no particular pattern for the purse clasp and hook.

Susan Jurasinski Cody *(See photo, page 117)*

On Susan's mother's side, the family is Norwegian. Her grandmother came from Søndre Land in Oppland and her great-grandfather was a *hallingdøl.* Susan's cousin from Enger purchased the bunad kit for her in Gjøvik. Her cousin and her grandmother embroidered the costume, and Susan sewed it herself with some help from Lizzie Riiber. This was quite an accomplishment. Susan is also thinking of acquiring a Hallingdal bunad in the future. She is the first of her family in the United States to own a bunad. She wanted to honor her grandmother by selecting a costume from her area of Norway. After Susan became a member of Sons of Norway, she began to research her genealogy, and she also became interested in bunads, which she studied through Husfliden's web sites.

Valdres bunad: *Ragnhild Fønhus Amble* *(See next page).*

OPPLAND

The Old Valdres Bunad for Women

There are several bunads from Valdres, but the old Valdres costume is probably the best known. This bunad has been in use for a long time. Hulda Garborg reconstructed it in 1914 in co-operation with Aksel Waldemar Johannesen and his wife Anne. Hulda Garborg was a pioneer in reviving interest in folk dancing. She also helped start the new bunad tradition. The Johannesen couple was also very much involved in the revival of interest in national costumes and culture in general. They were the founders of Heimen, a crafts and bunad store in Oslo.

The first reconstructed Valdres bunad had only embroidery on the apron and the bodice, not on the skirt. A broad pattern of embroidery was later added to the skirt (1948), and the embroidered apron was abandoned. The embroidery pattern was based on an old velvet hat from 1730, and on an old shawl from the district, but the cut of the bodice was based on a dress from the 1840's or 1850's. The embroidered purse was not part of the original costume, but later added on.

The blouse or shirt is made of white linen or cotton, with several embroidery patterns to choose from. The embroidery may be white or colored. One of the most popular shirts is a copy of an old model at Valdres Folk Museum. The bodice and skirt of the bunad are made of black or dark blue woolen broadcloth or tabby. The skirt is softly pleated. A red cotton underskirt with a pleated edge at the bottom gives the skirt a little bit more fullness. The bodice is heavily embroidered both in front and on the back. This costume comes with an embroidered cap, a cape or a pleated jacket based on an old model, black stockings and traditional black shoes.

All silver jewelry for this bunad is based on old dress silver from Valdres, which has a long and very rich silver tradition. Two *søljer* decorate the shirt, one for the collar with hanging attachments and a large one with rings and disks attached. In addition, there is a belt with silver attachments, a silver clasp for the purse, cuff links, and silver buckles for the shoes. Silver buttons or small hooks close the jacket.

Ragnhild Fønhus Amble *(See photo, page 119)*

Ragnhild was born in Valdres. Her bunad was a gift for her confirmation in 1945. Ragnhild says that the bunad tradition was very strong in Valdres, and every girl who could afford it, had a bunad made for her confirmation.

An aunt did the embroidery and a professional seamstress did the sewing. Ragnhild's bunad is black and has a vest with flaps in front and back. This is not seen often in new costumes today. Ragnhild was a member of a folk dancing group when she lived in Norway. Music was very much a part of the culture of her surroundings when she grew up.

Valdres bunads: *Vernette Pearson Karlsgodt and grandson Nathan Karlsgodt (See pages 122 and 126).*

The piano became her instrument of choice. She attended the Music Conservatory in Oslo for one year, and later she came to the United States where she finished a degree in music at San Diego State University, the same institution where her husband, Kjell, was a professor in the Theatre Department.

Vernette Pearson Karlsgodt *(See photo, page 121)*

Vernette's parents emigrated from Sweden and Finland. However, her husband Erling's family came from Valdres, and he wanted to give her a Valdres bunad. When they visited Norway in the fall of 2000, a kit for a Valdres costume was purchased in Fagernes. It was later assembled in San Diego. The Karlsgodt family also has some old parts of a Hardanger bunad that once was worn by Erling's sister.

Lizzie Skyllstad Riiber

The oldest version of the Valdres bunad was quite different from the two varieties available today. As mentioned previously, the Valdres bunad was first reconstructed around 1914. Lizzie inherited one of the oldest designs from her mother, whose family roots were in Valdres on her grandfather's side. This costume is probably at least eighty years old. It is made of soft, fine broadcloth, in a lighter blue shade than the ones made today. It has no embroidery on the skirt, which is pleated. However, the apron, which is also pleated, has very colorful embroidery in a fine wool thread. Among the several colors that are used, orange is the most striking. The apron has a large "rose" in each bottom corner. The bodice has this same embroidery motif in front and on the back. No purse came with this bunad as far as Lizzie knows, but there is an interesting old headdress, which may have been part of this costume. Diana Rem Rapallo, is posing in Lizzie's bunad. *(See photo next page)*

Joyce Wobermin Olsen *(See photo, page 125)*

The family of one of Joyce's grandfathers came from Moen, near Mosjøen in Nordland province. They arrived in this country as early as the 1850's and settled in Fairmont, Minnesota. Joyce was raised by her Norwegian grandfather, and his sister, Benedicta, who had no children of her own, also cared for her. It was under their influence that Joyce developed a real love and admiration for her Norwegian roots.

Joyce herself for a time lived in Norway with her Norwegian born husband, Sven. They traveled extensively and often visited the family cabin in Valdres, where Joyce learned to cross-country ski and fall down in the snow during Easter holidays. The wonderful memories that she developed in Valdres led her to adopt this region as her own

Valdres bunad: *Diana Rem Rapallo (See previous page).*

and to choose the traditional Valdres bunad. Joyce has served as Musician and Assistant Social Director in Valhall Lodge, and Sven is a past President.

Centes Kjensrud Wheeler *(See photo next page)*

All four of Centes' grandparents emigrated from Norway. Her father's father came from the Kjensrud farm in Valdres. Centes has many cousins in Norway, and she corresponds regularly with a cousin who still lives at Kjensrud. She has visited Valdres and other places from which her grandparents emigrated.

Centes owns the older version of the Valdres bunad. Her cousins in Valdres and Oslo helped her obtain a kit for the bunad in 1980. Several people in her community helped her finish the costume. In addition to the festive Valdres bunad, Centes also owns a blue and white everyday Valdres costume, acquired through Ann Hougen of El Cajon.

The Valdres Bunad for Men

The man's costume from Valdres which is shown in this book is about 80 years old. It came originally from Bagn in Valdres. It differs somewhat from the men's costumes which are in use today. It is made of fine black wool broadcloth. Jacket, pants and vest are all of the same color and fabric. The jacket is very short and fitted, as is the vest. The double-breasted jacket has a double row of six metal buttons. The jacket is worn open to show off the vest underneath. Double rows of eight smaller buttons decorate and close the vest.

The pants for this costume are long and with a slim cut. They are of a regular cut and do not have front flaps. The shirt for the costume is missing, so a regular bunad shirt was used for the picture.

Several bunads for men are available today in Valdres. They either have long pants or knee breeches. The costumes are made of black wadmel or wool broadcloth. The jacket is most often short, based on a *stutt-trøye,* short jacket, from the middle of the nineteenth century. The vests are often checked wool or plain red with black trim (Upper Valdres). The linen or cotton shirt has a stand-up collar. A silk scarf is tied around the neck. White woolen stockings are worn with the knee breeches, and tasseled garters also are used. Black bunad shoes and a black felt hat are part of the outfit. Except for the decorative buttons on the costume, a round silver pin is used to close the shirt at the neck and cuff links close the wristbands.

Valdres bunads: *Joyce Wobermin Olsen and Centes Kjensrud Wheeler (See pages 122 and 124).*

OPPLAND

Nathan Karlsgodt *(See photo, page 121)*

Nathan is wearing his great grandfather's 80-year-old costume. Olaf Karlsgodt came to the United States from Bagn in Valdres in 1899. Nathan's grandfather, Erling Karlsgodt, is now the owner of the costume, which most likely was made in Norway. Olaf wore this costume quite frequently. He was a very athletic man who could perform the famous *hallingkast* (a wheeling leap characteristic of the *halling* dance). He also placed well in a ski jump competition for men over 45 years of age. Nathan is posing with his grandmother, Vernette Karlsgodt, who also owns a Valdres bunad.

The Lundeby Bunad

This costume is closely associated with Lillehammer in Gudbrandsdalen. The painter Alf Lundeby designed it in 1935, perhaps in association with Helene Andersen. Lundeby wanted to use the colors of an old Norwegian coat of arms from around 1200, which had a golden lion on an orange red background. He chose an orange red wool fabric with the entire embroidery in yellow and gold tones. The bunad was also available in moss green with the same embroidery. Lundeby hoped that this would become a "national costume" for the whole country.

Because of its orange color, the bunad decreased in popularity during World War II. The color was associated with the flag of the Norwegian Nazi party. However, the bunad was significantly revised in the 1950's. The color is now either black, dark blue or white. The floral motifs are quite different from the original, especially on the skirt and purse. There are more similarities between the old and the new embroidery on the bodice.

The skirt of the costume is softly pleated, with a border of embroidery at its base. The bodice has embroidery both in front and on the back, and is closed by concealed hooks. The embroidered purse has either a brass or silver clasp. An embroidered small cap tops off the costume.

The blouse is of silk for the white costume, otherwise no special blouse is designed for this bunad. A jacket similar in cut to the Rondastakk jacket is worn with the Lundeby costume. Traditional bunad shoes and black stockings should be used, except with the white costume, which requires white stockings. The costume has no specially designed dress silver.

Rosalie Negaard Olson *(See photo next page)*

In Rosalie's family there are quite a few bunads, and in particular Lundeby bunads, also called Lillehammer bunads. Rosalie herself has

Lundeby bunads: *Rosalie Negaard Olson, Marit Olson Vincent and Jean Negaard Shogren* *(See pages 126-128).*

both a Hardanger bunad and a black Lundeby bunad. Jean Shogren, Rosalie's sister, made and gave the Lundeby bunad to her in 1994. Rosalie's mother had a Hardanger bunad. Rosalie's two sisters, one niece and her daughter all have Lundeby bunads. That makes quite a Lundeby show when they meet in festive attire!

Rosalie's bunad has the same flower pattern on the skirt as the original old orange red, and looks very different from the costume which is called a Lundeby bunad today. Lundeby himself designed both versions of the Lundeby costume. The colors of the embroidery on Rosalie's bunad have quite a bit of gold tones on the leaves and stems, but the flowers are basically in pastels.

Jean Negaard Shogren *(See photo above)*

About ten years ago Jean purchased a Lundeby, or Lillehammer, costume from a woman who contacted her Sons of Norway lodge, saying she had bought it from a cruise ship, which had used it for entertainment. She knew nothing about the dress, except that she thought it was pretty, but decided to sell it since she was not Norwegian and she had no place to wear it. The hat, purse and shirt were missing.

None of the bunad books Jean consulted showed this bunad, and she thought that it might have been created just for dancing on the cruise ship. Ann Hougen of El Cajon who owned Tradition, a business which among other services provided clients with bunad kits from Norway, created a purse and hat to match the dress. At the Norsk Høstfest in Minot, North Dakota, Jean and her husband, Everett, met a woman wearing a bunad with the same cut and design, but of red/orange wool and with all the embroidery in a gold color. She told them that her father had purchased her bunad in the 1950's, and that she considered it to be a Lillehammer bunad. Husfliden in Norway confirmed that Jean's costume was a Lillehammer bunad and sent a history of the dress. The age of Jean's costume is unknown. The bunad became the inspiration for the Lundeby costumes which Jean made for her sisters and two nieces.

Marit Olson Vincent *(See photo, page 127)*

Marit is the daughter of Rosalie and Donald Olson. She has a Hardanger bunad, and her Lundeby bunad is identical to the one owned by her mother, two aunts and cousin. The costume was given to her in 1995 by her aunt, Jean Shogren. Marit has visited Norway twice. The Shogren-Olson-Vincent team makes quite an impact when they show up in identical bunads, either Hardanger or Lundeby.

The Rondastakk

This very fine old bunad is the only costume from Gudbrandsdalen which has been in continuous use since the 1830's. The oldest costumes had a higher waistline and a longer skirt than today's bunad, but otherwise the present day bunad is much like the old costumes. The Rondastakk is especially used in the Otta Valley, in the northern part of Gudbrandsdalen. Unfortunately, it has had the misfortune of being copied in cotton and used by waitresses in restaurants. This tarnished its esteem somewhat. The Rondastakk is not work attire, but is to be used for festive occasions. Today a growing appreciation of this fact is fortunately taking place.

The name Rondastakk means striped skirt. There used to be a great variety of stripe patterns and color combinations, as well as many different check patterns for the bodice. Today many choices still remain, and many local districts have their own patterns and color combina-

Three generations in Rondastakk bunads: *Ingrid Bårdseng Lindgren, second from left, daughter Karin Lindgren Felkins, second from right and granddaughters Amanda Perricone, left, and Stefanie Perricone, right* *(See pages 130 and 132).*

tions. The softly pleated skirt has an extra fold of fabric above the hem, and further up on the skirt there is a pressed crease. The fabric is of two-shaft cotton and wool twill.

The bodice most often is in a checked red wool fabric, or may also be in plain red. Earlier it was also made of silk or damask. The bodice has a center seam in the back and curved seams on the sides. The checked patterns must meet correctly at the seams. Concealed hooks close the bodice in front. The skirt and bodice are attached.

Today most aprons are either in red or black wool with different horizontal stripes. A black embroidered silk apron may also be used. The shirt is either in cotton or linen with a small white decorative edging, either tatting or picot, on collar and cuffs. Of late a light blue shirt has also been introduced.

The most common headdress is a *stivaturklæ,* a starched white cotton head square. A dark embroidered silk cap is also available. The head square may have printed patterns in black or other colors.

A short wool jacket is used as an outer garment. The sleeves are wide with pleats at the shoulders, tapering off towards the wrists. Concealed hooks close the jacket. It is customary to use traditional black bunad shoes and black stockings with the bunad. No purse is used with this costume.

The silver ornaments for the costume consist of a collar button, one or two filigree *søljer,* often with attachments, cuff links and buckles for the shoes. All costumes in Gudbrandsdalen have silver pins on the shirt and not on the bodice.

Ingrid Bårdseng Lindgren *(See photo, page 129)*

Ingrid was born in Lillehammer. She emigrated in 1954 and settled in San Diego with her husband, Torfin. In Ingrid's family in Norway there were many bunads, in particular the Rondastakk costumes. The guides at Maihaugen Folk Museum in Lillehammer have traditionally worn the Rondastakk. As a girl, Ingrid always dreamt of being one of them. She did not become a guide, but she nevertheless acquired a Rondastakk.

It was natural for the women in Ingrid's family to wear a bunad on all festive occasions. Ingrid's family in San Diego has no fewer than four Rondastakk costumes and one Gudbrandsdalen festive bunad. Ingrid's bunad was given to her in 1970 by her sister, Liv. Ingrid inherited a Gudbrandsdalen *sølje* from her aunt. The pin is 70-80 years old. Ingrid has been very active in Valhall Lodge, Sons of Norway. She has served several terms as Social Director.

***Rondastakk bunads:** Elsa Ann Adams and June Nestingen Weller (See pages 132 and 134).*

OPPLAND

Karin Lindgren Felkins, Amanda and Stefanie Perricone *(See photo, page 129)*

When Karin visited Norway in 1960 as a three-year old girl, she was given her first Rondastakk. One can say she was initiated into her mother's women's club, the Bårdseng women's group, where everyone had a bunad. Karin used her bunad until she was twelve years old. Karin received a new costume in 1974, this time one in cotton. Her mother Ingrid sewed the costume.

Stefanie, Karin's daughter, was given a new Rondastakk in 1996. It came from Norway and is in wool. Amanda, Karin's youngest daughter, inherited her mother's first costume in 1996. There is a total of four Rondastakks in the Lindgren-Felkins-Perricone family. They represent three generations of the old Rondastakk tradition here in San Diego.

Amanda and Stefanie participated in the bunad show at the Sons of Norway convention in Anaheim in 1998. They also use their costumes for ethnic fairs at their school. Their mother, Karin, participated in the Rolling Trolls folk dance group in San Diego when she was a teenager. Of course all of the ladies in the extended Lindgren family dress up in their bunads for May 17th. In this picture, Karin is wearing Lizzie Riiber's Rondastakk.

Elka Ann Adams

When Elka was elected to be queen of the House of Norway, she purchased a Rondastakk with the title money. It was purchased thirteen years ago as a kit from Norway. Ellen Holk sewed the costume for her. It has been used at many functions both at the House of Norway and Valhall Lodge. Elka also brought her bunad with her when she went to Norway to study and work as an au pair. In 1993 she wore her Rondastakk in a May 17 parade in Norway!

Elka's mother, Jacqueline Lyngen Adams, has a Norwegian family background. When her children were young, she purchased fabric, and Ann Hougen of El Cajon sewed costumes for her three daughters and son. She has four girls' and a boy's costume. The children were much involved in Scandinavian dance troupes, May 17th parades, ethnic school projects, as well as being queens and princesses of the House of Norway. They always wore their costumes at these functions. Elsa, Elka's sister, was Queen of the House of Norway for the year 2001, and she is posing in her sister's bunad. *(See photo, page 131)*

Rondastakk bunads: *June Johnson and Mari Olson Rem (See next page).*

OPPLAND

June Nestingen Weller *(See photo, page 131)*

June's Norwegian ancestors came from the Nestingen farm in Øyer, Gudbrandsdalen. The whole family emigrated to America between 1869 and 1904, eventually ending up in Coon Valley, Wisconsin. Since there were nine children in the family, the Nestingen tree has spread its branches far and wide in the United States.

June purchased her Rondastakk in 1995. "I wanted a bunad in memory of my beloved grandmother, who had passed away," is how June explains why she obtained a Rondastakk. Her sister, Lorraine, who lives in Westby, Wisconsin, a stronghold of Norwegian culture according to June, helped her acquire the costume. Lorraine ordered the kit and did the sewing. As far as June knows, she is the first in her family to own a bunad.

House of Norway

The House of Norway owns a Rondastakk in addition to the man's Voss bunad previously mentioned. The Rondastakk has often been used by members to represent House of Norway at special functions. The bodice is red with a large checked pattern, and the skirt is striped. June Johnson, a member of House of Norway and past President of Ladies of Valhall, Valhall Lodge # 25, Sons of Norway, is shown wearing the costume with a white Hardanger apron, also owned by the House of Norway. *(See photo, page 133)*

Mari Olson Rem *(See photo, page 133)*

Both of Mari's parents had their roots in Gudbrandsdalen. Her father's parents were from the Sjoa area near Otta, and her mother's family came from Gausdal. Mari acquired her Rondastakk in 1984. She purchased a kit from a local dealer and made it herself. Her bunad is in cotton, "an everyday bunad," as she terms it herself. Her costume has a striped skirt with a solid red bodice. The apron is black.

When Mari bought her Rondastakk, she wanted a bunad to honor her Norwegian family roots. This year she also acquired a Gudbrandsdalen festive costume. Mari has been a very active member in several Norwegian-American organizations over the years.

Charlotte Falck Nielsen *(See photo next page)*

Charlotte acquired her Rondastakk in about 1975 when she and her husband visited Oslo. Her husband, S. Falck Nielsen, was born in Norway and served for many years as Honorary Norwegian Consul in San Diego. They were both active in Sons of Norway and other Norwegian organizations in the area. Charlotte used her bunad when she, together with

Rondastakk bunad: *Charlotte Falck Nielsen* *(See previous page).*

her husband, represented Norway on special occasions.

Inger Somdalen Olson *(No photo)*

Inger's Rondastakk was purchased in 1980 from Husfliden in Oslo. Since she had become a member of Sons of Norway the year before, she knew the costume would be used often. Her bunad is in wool and has a checked bodice. She also has the traditional silver jewelry to go with the Rondastakk. In addition to this bunad, Inger has an Oslo costume. Both Inger and her husband, Roy, have been very active in Sons of Norway, both in their own lodge and on a wider basis.

Lizzie Skyllstad Riiber

Lizzie's Rondastakk is from 1973. Her family owned a log cabin in Vestre Gausdal, and her father-in-law used to minister in the summertime in the churches of Vestre (Western) and Østre (Eastern) Gausdal. The people in the area went to church in their bunads for special occasions like christenings and weddings. Therefore it was natural for Lizzie to purchase a bunad from Husfliden in Lillehammer for use in church. The fabric in the *stakk* (skirt) is hand woven *verken* (cotton and wool twill), and plant dyed. The bodice is made of red wool damask. Every Midsummer Eve the family went to Maihaugen Folk Museum in Lillehammer to take part in the celebration of the longest day of the year, with *rømmegrøt* (sour cream porridge), *flatbrød,* folk dancing and singing. "The atmosphere in the midst of the old timber houses, shining like gold in the romantic sunset, with everyone in their bunads and white shirts in the dim Nordic light night, is something that I still experience every time I dress in my Rondastakk." Karin Felkins is wearing Lizzie's bunad in the Lindgren-Felkins family picture in this book.
(See photo, page 129)

The Graffer Bunad

This bunad is based on an old blue, richly embroidered skirt from the 1700's, found at the Graffer farm in Lom, Gudbrandsdalen. Several other single colored wool skirts with much embroidery have been found in this district, dating back to the 1700's. The one from Graffer is a particularly handsome example. Unfortunately, the bodice was missing. When it was first copied in the 1930's, an embroidered bodice was used. However, in 1952 the Graffer family and the Gudbrandsdalen husflidsforening (Home Craft Association) came up with a single colored bodice, based on other finds in the district. The result was a bunad with a blue, softly pleated embroidered skirt in woolen tabby. Many colored wool yarns as well as metallic threads are used for the embroidery.

Graffer bunad: *Lael Kovtun* *(See next page).*

A red or green brocade bodice of the same cut as the Rondastakk is wornd today. The bodice is meant to be hand sewn and closed by four or five concealed hooks. It is attached to the skirt. A green or red underskirt with a large pocket is used with this costume.

The cap and purse are of the same material as the skirt, with wool embroidery patterned from the skirt. The shirt is a copy of one found at Graffer. It is in white linen, with a stand-up collar and cuffs embroidered in white. Another shirt, used for other costumes in the district, may also be worn. Black stockings and bunad shoes are part of this outfit. There is also a jacket of the same fabric as the skirt, quite like the Rondastakk jacket.

The bunad jewelry in Gudbrandsdalen is most often decorated with filigree. A collar button with attachments, a large heart shaped pin also with attachments, cuff links and the purse clasp are all in silver, although the latter may also be made of brass. In addition there are other types of pins or *søljer* in use in Gudbrandsdalen, and all may be used with this bunad.

Ann Stokke Hougen

When in Norway in 1977, Ann bought the kit for a Graffer bunad. Since she is quite an accomplished seamstress and embroiderer, she finished the costume herself. Over the years it has been used both by Ann and her sister Glenda. They have also "shared" other bunads. They have in their possession a Rogaland, a Vest-Telemark, a Graffer and a white Bergen bunad, all of them made by Ann. Lael Kovtun of La Jolla is posing in the Graffer bunad. *(See photo, page 137)*

The Gudbrandsdalen Festive Bunad

In 1922 Aksel Waldemar Johannesen discovered a beautiful old embroidered skirt or *stakk* from Gudbrandsdalen. Today this skirt is at the Norwegian Folk Museum at Bygdøy in Oslo. Many folk costumes or parts of such were preserved in Gudbrandsdalen. Some of the women's costumes had embroidery. However, the reconstructions of the folk costumes which took place in the 1920's were much inspired by Hulda Garborg's idea of what a modern bunad should look like. She was very much in favor of wool embroidery, not only on the bodice or skirt, but on the whole outfit. Johannessen and his wife Anna worked closely with Hulda on several bunads, and were influenced by her. The floral embroidery on the skirt was therefore copied on bodice, cap and purse. An apron was added with the same embroidery. In the old days not all costumes in Gudbrandsdalen had an apron or purse, but some did, and today one has the choice of wearing an apron or not.

Gudbrandsdalen festbunad: *Aase Gun Pedersen Bence (See next page).*

Oppland

The softly pleated skirt and bodice of this costume are either in black or blue woolen tabby or broadcloth. Earlier white was also an option. The embroidered apron may be in black or blue wool or black silk. The embroidered cap is in wool, but earlier it was also made of silk. The short bodice has the same shape as the bodice of the Rondastakk. It is attached to the skirt, and embroidered both in front and on the back. Concealed hooks are used to close the bodice in front, but the top is kept open.

The shirt is either in linen or cotton with a down-turned collar. Both the collar and cuffs are edged with tatting. Traditional black shoes and black stockings are worn with the costume. A short wool jacket, of the same cut as the jacket for the Rondastakk, is worn as an outer garment.

The silver jewelry for this bunad consists of a large filigree *sølje* and a collar button, or a smaller *sølje* instead of the collar button. The cuff links are also in filigree. The purse clasp is in silver or brass.

Aase Gun Pedersen Bence *(See photo, page 139)*

Aase comes from Hisøy near Arendal. She emigrated in 1970. Her bunad is from 1995. Her mother bought the kit for her bunad from Husfliden in Lillehammer. Aase did the beautiful embroidery herself, but had some help sewing the costume.

Only a few of Aase's relatives in Norway have bunads. She chose the Gudbrandsdalen festive bunad because it was the one she liked the most. This bunad is very popular in eastern Norway (Østlandet), also among people who do not live in Gudbrands-dalen. Aase's costume is dark blue, and she does not have an apron.

Mari Olson Rem *(See photo next page)*

Mari acquired her brand new Gudbrandsdalen festive bunad in the fall of 2001. This bunad was an easy choice for her since all her grandparents' families were born in the Gudbrandsdalen Valley. "My paternal grandmother emigrated at age 18 from Sjoa to the United States in 1877. Grandfather Edward Skrefsrud was born in Lillehammer and moved with his family to La Crosse County, Wisconsin, in 1872, when he was 14. The family later took the name Olson. The old Skrefsrud house is now part of the Maihaugen outdoor museum in Lillehammer. A large statue of Lars Skrefsrud stands in the churchyard in Lillehammer. Lars was Mari's grandfather's uncle and founded the Santal Ebenezer Mission in Bengal, India."

Another great-grandfather, Johan Torgerson Trinrud, lived in Østre Gausdal. He came to the United States in 1857 and settled in Scandinavia, Wisconsin. Mari's grandfather, Albert, was born there and married Martha Gudlien Sødersteen.

Gudbrandsdalen festbunad: *Mari Olson Rem and Karin Lindgren Felkins (See pages 140 and 142).*

According to Mari, four ladies were instrumental in helping her acquire her costume:

Anne Kløvnes Høidal contacted Husfliden in Lillehammer, which sent brochures, prices and pertinent information.

Lizzie Riiber located a young lady who embroidered the bunad. Lizzie also helped in many other ways.

Anne-Lise Gustavsen from Tønsberg, Norway, embroidered the bunad in record time and did a perfect job.

Dale Roybal was the seamstress and is getting to be somewhat of an expert in constructing bunads.

Mari is very grateful for the help she received in obtaining her new festive attire. She wears her bunad with a great deal of pride.

Karin Lindgren Felkins *(See photo, page 141)*

Karin comes from a family with very strong bunad traditions. Her parents, Torfin and Ingrid Lindgren, were born and raised in Norway. Most members of her mother's family, including Karin herself, own a Rondastakk, but Karin also has a black Gudbrandsdalen festive bunad. She inherited the bunad from her mother's sister, aunt Gunvor Bårdseng Hansen, who in turn had inherited it from her aunt, Gunhild Bårdseng. The costume was embroidered some time in the 1920's. The embroidery yarn was plant dyed. The costume was hand carried by her aunt's husband and delivered to Karin when he visited San Diego after his wife had passed away.

Florence L. Borstad Hiepler *(See photo next page)*

Adolph Borstad, Forence's father, was born in Blaker (Romerike) in Norway and her mother's parents came from Vang in Valdres. In 1970 her husband surprised her with a Gudbrandsdalen festive costume as a birthday present. He chose this bunad because he thought it was very beautiful. Husfliden in Oslo had it made professionally. Six different women worked on the costume. As far as Florence knows, she is the only one in her family in the United States who owns a bunad.

Gudbrandsdalen Embroidered Cotton Bunad

This costume comes in bright red, dark red, or blue. The skirt is in the basic color of the costume, but with contrasting stripes. The single colored attached bodice is embroidered with small flowers, with yellow and gold as the dominant colors. The apron has the same embroidery as the bodice. A cotton blouse with tatting is worn with the bunad. The same jewelry that enhance other costumes in Gudbrandsdalen can be used with this bunad as well.

Gudbrandsdalen festbunad: *Florence L. Borstad Hiepler (See previous page).*

Gudbrandsdalen embroidered and everyday bunads: *Christina Becker Jenkins and Louise Hofheimer (See pages 145).*

Christina (Tina) Becker Jenkins *(See photo previous page)*
In 1997 Tina purchased her bunad from a dealer in Minnesota. It originally came from a bunad dealer in Norway. Tina is of Norwegian descent and "loves the thought of the tradition" behind her bunad. When her daughter is older, Tina will pass her costume on to her. Tina has served as Treasurer of the House of Norway and wears her bunad on the organization's festive occasions.

Louise Hofheimer *(See photo previous page)*
Louise has no family connections with Norway, but as part of a Scandinavian dance group in San Diego, she wanted an outfit that was suitable for dancing in a warm climate. She chose this cotton costume from Gudbrandsdalen, which she is very happy to own. She has some beautiful bunad silver from Gudbrandsdalen to wear with her costume. Louise's costume was purchased in November 2000 from a dealer in Wisconsin.

HEDMARK

The Østerdalen Bunad for Men

The folk costumes worn by men in Østerdalen did not go out of use until well after the start of the 20th century. This is quite interesting since the folk costume tradition for men weakened much earlier than the tradition for women in most districts. In Østerdalen the reverse seems true. The present day bunad was revised between 1981 and 1986. It was given very favorable reviews, among others by the Norwegian Bunad and Folk Costume Board, which stated that this model is a true copy of costumes worn in this area between 1830 and 1880.

There are two linen or cotton shirts to choose from for this costume. One is based on an elaborately embroidered bridegroom's shirt; the other is much simpler. The wool vest has a double row of buttons, a total of twenty buttons. It has a narrow stand-up collar and lapels. The color is either checkered black and red, or reddish-brown or green with a printed pattern.

The pants are knee breeches of black wadmel with a front flap, closed by six rather large buttons. Five smaller buttons are placed by each knee for decoration. Buckles below the knees close the breeches. Moose leather was often used for the breeches in the old days. The supply of this leather was never any problem in Østerdalen. Even today there is an abundant moose population in this valley, and moose

Østerdalen bunad: *Ola Brevig (See next page).*

breeches have experienced a revival.

Like the breeches, the jacket is made of black wadmel. It has a stand-up collar and flat lapels. The short jacket has a double row of six large buttons in front and two on each sleeve. It is worn open. A small neck scarf is in silk. There are many different scarves to choose from. Stockings are knitted from white thin wool yarn, or they may be white with black rose patterns. They are held in place by plaited, many colored garters. Black bunad shoes are worn traditionally. Notice the very particular peaked black cap, called Østerdalen cap *(østerdalslue)*. A knitted red wool cap was often worn earlier and is still quite popular. The buckles and all the buttons for this costume used to be in brass. In earlier times, very little silver was used in Østerdalen. Today buckles and buttons are frequently cast in bronze. A small silver collar button and cuff links are often the only silver accompanying this costume.

Ola Brevig *(See photo previous page)*

After a family reunion at Elverum Museum in 1982, Ola decided to purchase a bunad. Many of the men came to the reunion in this particular bunad, and most of the women wore bunads from various districts. Ola was raised in Østerdalen and Oslo and feels a strong affinity with the southern part of Østerdalen where his father's family lives. This costume was therefore a natural choice. It was made in Elverum by experts. Ola's costume has brass buttons, and he wears a small sølje. The bunad tradition in his family is alive and well.

Ola has been very active in several Norwegian-American associations, but in particular Sons of Norway, where he has been President of Valhall Lodge #25. In addition, he has served as Sons of Norway's International Treasurer, International Director and President of District Six. This has given him ample opportunity to work for and represent his heritage. He wears his bunad proudly at the many festive occasions in which he participates.

Akershus

The Romerike Bunad

There are few old descriptions of folk costumes from Akershus province. Its local traditions were probably influenced quite early by city fashions from Oslo. However, some old descriptions and drawings do exist, and these, together with old pieces of clothing, provide an idea of what folk costumes looked like in earlier times. Today there are several women's festive costumes representing Romerike. Reconstruction of the first bunad from this district started in the 1920's. The result, which didn't include any embroidery, did not catch on. It was not before 1932, when an old embroidered purse from the late 1700's was found and subsequently became the basis for an embroidered bunad, that a popular costume was developed. The embroidery pattern was used for the bodice and skirt as well as the apron, the cap and, of course, the purse. The cut of the bodice is based on a model from 1760-80. This new bunad as we see it today was finished in 1940. Two other festive bunads for Romerike have been reconstructed, one in 1946 and the other in 1955.

The color choices for this bunad are blue, red or blue-green. The fabric is woolen tabby. The skirt is gathered in soft pleats and attached to a narrow waistband. The skirt is then stitched to the bodice, which is closed by three hooks and clasps. The apron is often of the same fabric as the rest of the costume and has the same type of wool embroidery in three shades of yellow and one of red. Embroidered linen aprons or linen aprons with printed patterns are also in use.

The costume comes with a choice of two embroidered white linen shirts. A short jacket or a long cape is the outer garment. The cap, which is a copy of an old one, is made in the same fabric as the rest of the costume. It is embroidered and decorated with a narrow lace trim in front. White stockings are recommended for this costume. As with all other bunads, traditional shoes should be used. They are an important part of a bunad.

The silver pins *(søljer)* for the bunad are heart-shaped with different attachments. In addition, cuff links, hooks, a purse clasp and a belt with silver attachments are part of the jewelry. Earrings, which were not part of traditional folk costume finery, are frequently used today. The large heart-shaped *sølje (romerikssølja)* is fastened at the neck opening of the shirt. It is a copy of one from the 1700's found in the district. The monogram of King Christian VII is seen at the top of the pin.

Hege Kristin Larsen Hagen *(See photo next page)*

"From Norway with love" is how Hege Kristin ended up in San Diego. She married her husband, Neil Lance Hagen, of Norwegian descent in the old Torpo church in Heidal, Gudbrandsdalen. This is the area her husband's paternal grandparents came from in the late 1890's. The wedding party was held at Harildstad Søre in a building from the 1750's. "We felt we were closing a cirle, coming back to his family's starting point," is how Hege Kristin describes their feelings. She wore her red Romerike bunad for her wedding dress, topped off with a small bridal crown.

Romerike bunad: *Hege Kristin Larsen Hagen (See previous page).*

Hege Kristin comes from the Romerike area and grew up in Lørenskog. Although most of her female family members in Norway have a Vest-Oppland costume, Hege Kristin selected a Romerike bunad because it represented her home district. As a girl, Hege Kristin also wore a Vest-Oppland bunad.

The Romerike bunad was given to Hege Kristin in 1992 as a token of appreciation for work she had done over several years. "To me it was a fantastic gift, which I treasure greatly. Wearing my bunad makes me feel proud and well dressed. In Norway it is considered an appropriate dress for all kinds of festive occasions." Kari Lystad from Romerike made the bunad. She did both the embroidery and sewing. The silver was purchased from a local jeweler in Lørenskog.

Rhonda Addington Brevig *(See photo next page)*

In 2000 Rhonda received her bunad as a gift from her mother-in-law, Karin Brevig. Karin made the costume, which was finished in 1953. She used it for many years before it was given to her daughter-in-law. Rhonda is married to Kenneth Brevig, whose parents were both born in Norway. Most women from Karin's family in Norway have a Romerike bunad, which represents the district where Karin came from. Both Rhonda and Kenneth are active in Sons of Norway.

Kianna Liv Brevig *(See photo next page)*

Kianna, age four, is the daughter of Rhonda and Kenneth Brevig. She is posing in a Romerike bunad, which originally was made for her aunt, Sidsel Brevig, when she was about five years old. Grandmother Karin Brevig made the costume. Kianna is the third generation of the Brevig family in San Diego with a Romerike bunad.

ØSTFOLD

The Østfold Bunad

In the 1930's the Østfold Home Craft Association started a drive to research the folk costume traditions in the province, with the intention of reconstructing a bunad. The costume was presented in 1936. It was a long time since folk costumes as such had been used in this area, and the surviving material was basically from the early 1800's, inspired by the Rococo fashion of the late 1700's and early 1800's.

The skirt is based on one from Ellefsrød in Idd (southeast of Halden). It is in black woolen tabby and softly pleated. It has a two centimeter green

Romerike bunads: *Rhonda Addington Brevig and daughter Kianna Liv Brevig* *(See previous page).*

or rusty red border at the hem with a red stitching above it. An underskirt in the same color as the bodice is used with the costume.

The bodice is either green or rusty red, made of hand woven wool damask with a pattern of stylized fir trees. The model for the bodice came from Berg near Halden. It is closed by eyelets and a long silver chain. A black belt with a green or rusty red stripe is part of the outfit. A white linen shirt with shirred neck and a stand-up collar is embroidered in Renaissance fashion in counted threadwork. It is based on an 1840's original.

The black silk shawl is copied from one found at Ellefsrød in Idd. The original was bought in Valdres in the 1880's. The embroidery from the shawl is also used on the cap and purse. The original shawl had two different color versions of the same motif, one in red and one in green. The green version was chosen. Two opposite corners of the shawl have this colorful festive embroidery; the two others have "a flower of mourning" in silver grey and blue, to be used to show sorrow.

The purse is in black wool with an embroidered flower motif from the shawl. The clasp is based on an old model from Onsøy. The cap is in black silk with the same embroidery as the shawl. Black stockings and black bunad shoes with heart shaped silver buckles are used for the Østfold bunad. Other shoe buckles are also available. A black short reversible wool cape is used as an outer garment. It is lined in either green or rusty red, depending on the color of the bodice, and closed by a silver or brass clasp.

The jewelry consists of a purse clasp, a silver chain and eyelets, a heart shaped small pin to close the shirt, a large heart shaped *sølje*, two heart shaped pins to keep the shawl in place, cuff links, and a heart shaped buckle for the belt. Silver attachments cover the whole belt. The dress silver is based on antique pieces.

May-Eivor Belsby Espinosa *(See photo next page)*

May-Eivor's bunad was made by her mother after World War II when she attended Risum School of Home Economics. Her mother used it all her life, and when she passed away, May-Eivor inherited it. The costume has a green low cut bodice. May-Eivor has all the required parts of the bunad, including a cape, but not a cap. All her silver jewelry is inherited. Since her family comes from Varteig in Østfold, it is not surprising that she has a very old Swedish *sølje*, as well as a Norwegian one which is over 100 years old. In addition to the traditional pieces, May-Eivor also has a silver belt, which has become popular in more recent times.

***Østfold bunad:** May-Eivor Belsby Espinosa (See previous page).*

Oslo

The Oslo Costume

The costume originated in 1947. Many cities in Norway, and in particular Oslo, lost their contact with local folk costume tradition quite early. Cities were by and large influenced by European fashions. However, when great interest for the old folk costumes and the desire to be part of a bunad tradition dramatically increased after World War II, Oslo also wanted a festive attire to call its own. Oslo's largest department store, Steen & Strøm, decided to create a costume for Oslo's 900-year celebration in 1950 and the store's own 150th anniversary.

The costume has a pleated light blue woolen broadcloth skirt, a fitted bodice, a cape, a cap and purse, all in the same fabric. The skirt has a light grey panel at the bottom decorated with embroidered wild flowers, which spill over the grey panel onto the blue of the skirt. The flowers are meant to represent the wild flowers of Oslomarka, the beloved large nature preserve around the city. The same flower motif is used on the bodice and cap. The purse has another embroidery pattern, one that depicts the patron saint of Oslo, Saint Halvard. The legend has it that he was wounded trying to rescue a woman and subsequently drowned with a millstone around his neck. In spite of the millstone, the body would not sink, so Halvard was declared a saint. He is depicted on the purse with a millstone in one hand and an arrow in the other.

The costume comes with a pearl grey silk or cotton blouse. The cape is very long and reaches down to the grey panel of the skirt. The Oslo costume has specially designed shoes to go with it. At first traditional bunad silver was worn with the costume. Today there is jewelry especially designed for the costume. The inspiration for the new design was the wild flowers used in the embroidery pattern on the dress. The jewelry consists of a large and a small *sølje,* earrings, a ring, cuff links, a belt clasp and attachments for a silver belt, and a purse clasp. The silver belt is a recent addition to the finery. A headband is now available for those who prefer that instead of the cap or as an alternative.

Kristine Olsen Davis *(See photo next page)*

Aasta Elstad Olsen, her fraternal grandmother, gave Kristine her Oslo costume. Aasta came from Eisletta in Namdalen, but settled in Oslo as a very young woman. Her husband, Ivar Olsen, was a missionary in Korea after World War II, where he helped build orphanages and a hospital. On one of his trips back to Oslo, he decided to buy his wife and daughter, Laila, each a bunad. It was not easy to acquire a bunad in a

Oslo bunad:
Kristine Olsen Davis
(See previous page).

hurry, and he wanted the costumes in his suitcase when he left. So he happened to see a beautiful costume, the Oslo costume, at the Steen & Strøm department store. This was the one he bought for his wife and daughter. Ivar himself was an Oslo man, and Aasta had lived in Oslo for many years, so the choice was quite a natural one.

Berit Torpenberg Austin Funnemark *(See photo, page 157)*

In 1957 Berit and her family emigrated from Oslo. Berit's mother acquired her Oslo costume when she was in Norway on a vacation in the late 1970's or early 1980's. When she died in 1990, the costume was passed on to Berit. Since Berit inherited the costume, she has added a

***Oslo bunad:** Berit Torpenberg Austin Funnemark (See page 155).*

cape, a headband and a silver belt with the new design.

The first costume Berit owned was a red everyday costume from Gudbrandsdalen. It was given to her even before her mother purchased her own Oslo costume. Several of Berit's relatives in Norway have bunads of different kinds.

Elisabet Ohnstad Harth *(No photo)*

Elisabet was born and raised in Oslo. She came to the United States in 1981. She is the owner of an Oslo drakt which she inherited from her old Sunday school teacher, Dagny Johanesen. Dagny made the costume in the 1950's. Elisabet's mother has a costume from Sogn. From her grandmother, Elisabet has a few *søljer* also from Sogn, where her grandparents lived.

Jeanette Olsen Kurz *(See photo, page 158)*

Both of Jeanette's parents were born in Norway. Her mother came from Farsund, Lista, and her father from Åkerøy, an island near Lillesand. They both came to this country as young people. Jeanette's father was a Norwegian seaman who decided to go ashore in the United States. He settled in Brooklyn, New York, where he met his Norwegian wife.

The first bunad Jeanette owned was a Hardanger bunad. In 1988 she decided on an Oslo bunad as well, and hired Ann Hougen of "Tradition" in El Cajon to make the costume. Jeanette has been very active in Sons of Norway since she was very young. She was a member in Brooklyn, and in San Diego both her husband Bob and Jeanette are members of Valhall Lodge, where Bob has served as President and Jeanette was Publicity Director from 1987 to 1992.

Inger Somdalen Olson *(See photo, page 159)*

"I am proud of my Norwegian heritage, and therefore I enjoy wearing my bunad, a symbol of my heritage." Inger's first bunad was given to her when she was seventeen years old. She inherited an old Hardanger bunad, which she used for many years until her daughter took it over. Her next bunad was a Rondastakk, and the last one is an Oslo drakt or costume. Inger was the first in her family to own a bunad. She is also an Oslo girl, so choosing an Oslo costume was very natural for her. Her outfit was made in 1984, and Inger has had ample opportunity to wear her festive costumes since both she and her husband, Roy Olson, have been very active in Sons of Norway since 1979 when they became members. Inger has served as Vice President, Social Director and Cultural Director of her lodge. Roy has served as President of District 6, Sons of Norway. In addition, he has held many other offices in the organization.

Oslo bunad: *Jeanette Olsen Kurz (See page 157).*

Oslo bunad: *Inger Somdalen Olson (See page 157).*

SILJE

The Silje Costume

(The Silje Festdrakt)

This is a very attractive modern festdrakt, a costume based on some folk costume traditions, but much more loosely than most other bunads. It does not have any ties to a particular area, and does not claim to be based on any specific folk costume tradition.

The Silje costume has the same basic cut as many bunads dating back to the second half of the nineteenth century. It is made of dark green, blue, or black wool fabric. It consists of a skirt with soft pleats, an attached bodice, a purse, belt and large shawl. Prominent floral embroidery in several colors, mainly red, blue, yellow and greens, decorate the whole outfit. The shawl, belt, and bottom of the skirt also have double wavy lines in yellow embroidery. Silver eyelets and a long silver chain close the fitted bodice.

The shirt is a traditional bunad shirt. It is white or off-white, with an embroidered stand-up collar and cuffs. Berge M. Bertelsen, Hommersåk, especially designed the silver jewelry for this festdrakt. The oxidized silver jewelry has a "wild rose" design and consists of a collar button, a larger square *sølje,* hooks and chain for the bodice, a two part belt buckle and cuff links. Earrings, a shawl pin, a ring and a circular *sølje* are also made in the same design as the basic silver pieces.

Tamara Tow Stautland *(See photo next page)*

Tamara started thinking of buying a bunad ten years ago. She did quite a bit of research with the intention of making her own, perhaps a Rogaland bunad. Her paternal great grandfather, who came to the United States in 1883, was from Rogaland. Her great grandmother on her father's side was also Norwegian. Here in San Diego, Tamara met another Norwegian, Professor Sigurd Stautland from Bergen, whom she married.

Since the task of making her own bunad seemed rather daunting, Tam selected a Silje costume, which she found very attractive. She had it made by a mother-daughter team of bunad experts in Oslo. Tam and her husband are very active in the Norwegian-American community. Sigurd has served as President of Valhall Lodge.

Mary Tellefsen Jacobsen *(See photo next page)*

Mary was born in Norway. She emigrated in 1946 with her family. In Brooklyn, New York, she met a Norwegian-American, Adolf (Jake)

***Silje festdrakt:** Tamara Tow Stautland and Mary Tellefsen Jacobsen (See previous page).*

Jacobsen, a naval officer. They married and eventually settled in San Diego after having moved many times because of Jake's career. In San Diego they both joined Sons of Norway, the House of Norway and other Norwegian-American organizations. Jake is President of the Norwegian Fish Club in San Diego.

After having found out that it would take three to four years at least to acquire an Aust-Agder bunad, Mary purchased her Silje festdrakt in July 2000 when she was in Norway. Mary and Jake are the lucky owners of Mary's childhood home in Tvedestrand (Holt), where they spend all their summers.

In 1959 Mary's mother gave her granddaughter, Irene, a beautiful child's bunad in wool. It was purchased at Husfliden in Arendal. This bunad was worn by Irene, her younger sister Beverly, and is now worn by Beverly's daughter, Alexandra.

Tordis Gundersen Kostic *(No photo)*

Tordis grew up in Oslo, but immigrated to the United States in 1956. She acquired her blue Silje costume in the fall of 2000. Her blouse has a beautiful cutout pattern on the collar and cuffs. Tordis has an old *sølje* which was given to her 60 years ago. Her son, Alex, persuaded her to purchase a bunad. He feels "that by owning a bunad I will always have a proper dress for May 17 and other Norwegian celebrations that I attend." There are several bunads in Tordis' family in Norway, and among these are costumes both from Romerike and Hardanger.

CHAPTER III

When to Wear Your Bunad and How to Take Care of It

TOP OF PAGE: Embroidery detail on Hardanger apron from Gjøa Olsdatter Jordal. Contributed by Myrtle Whitworth, her granddaughter.

WHILE WORKING ON THIS BUNAD PROJECT, I have received several questions about when it is appropriate to wear a bunad. Since a bunad is a Norwegian costume, we may consider what is the custom in Norway today concerning this question. I would like to quote what the Norwegian Bunad and Folk Dress Board has to say: "In the old days when people wore their folk costumes, they didn't wear their best clothing except at special occasions and on feast days. Everyday clothing was worn during the workweek. In the same way, it is natural today to wear your festbunad for festive occasions and holidays, as well as for a gala. However, remember you are not automatically well dressed in a bunad. To look right, your bunad must be made of quality materials and have a proper fit. All parts of the outfit should be worn, and your costume must be properly taken care of."

As mentioned above, where separate outfits exist in a bunad district for work and for festive occasions, these must be used appropriately. Obviously an everyday work costume should not be worn at a gala event. Also, if there is a difference between a married and an unmarried woman's costume, such variations should be taken into account. For many districts, however, only one type of costume exists, the one for festive occasions, and similarly, for many bunads no distinction is made between a married and an unmarried woman.

So what are these special occasions mentioned above that we are talking about? If we look at tradition and at how it is followed in Norway today, we would include baptisms, confirmations, weddings, and any important anniversary. In the old days, people would wear their best church outfits for funerals as well. Some costumes would have certain colors for mourning on some garments or certain details added to a garment. For instance, shawls could have different embroidery for sorrow or feast, and the way the shawl was folded would show the appropriate triangle. These differences have for the most part disappeared, although some costumes still hold on to the old tradition. The modern bunad tradition is also so closely connected to festive and joyful events that very few would feel comfortable wearing a bunad to a funeral. In the still very traditional bunad areas the case is different. There you may see people in church wearing their bunads, also for funerals. In the old days one's very best clothing was worn on the most important church days.

Very old handmade filigree neck button with large tassel, most likely from Valdres. Interited by Lizzie Riiber from great grandfather, Hans Andersen, born 1859. Contributed by Lizzie Riiber.

Other occasions that today call for dressing up in your festive bunad would be any gala, 17th of May, Christmas, important birthdays, and any event when you want to emphasize your Norwegian affiliation or heritage. Many people both in Norway and abroad will wear bunads for big family reunions. It is also customary to dress in a bunad for any event in connection with folk dancing and folk music, especially if you participate. Most people will automatically know when it is appropriate to wear a bunad. Of course, nobody wants to feel out of place, but by using your own discretion and some sensible guidelines, you will do what is customary and appropriate.

A bunad or festdrakt today is a big investment in monetary terms. If you have made it yourself, both time and money are involved, not to mention the sentimental values that are attached to any costume. The older a bunad is, the more precious it becomes, and the more carefully it should be looked after. If it is inherited, it may represent both the work and cultural values of women in your family. Sometimes several generations have left their mark on one single costume. The oldest costumes are usually less standardized, and therefore have more individuality than our modern costumes. The personal stamp may be stronger on the older costumes. All bunads have a history.

The first requirement that a new bunad owner needs to know is how to store it. Do not use a plastic bag. There are many different natural fibers in a bunad. They need to breathe. If you have a chance, hang your costume outdoors, but out of the sunshine, for a few hours after use, or let it air indoors. Check to see that it is clean. Small spots can be carefully removed, but otherwise a reputable drycleaner is recommended. It is also recommended that the garment be turned inside out with the bodice hanging inside. Fasten a couple of loops on the waistband and hang it on a hanger. Because the garment is quite heavy, this is better than just hanging it on a hanger and thereby stretching the bodice. Place the bunad in a cotton garment bag. You can easily make one yourself from an old sheet, or purchase one for a very reasonable price. Close the bag carefully. Many people also store their costume wrapped in a sheet and placed in a drawer. That is fine too, but if it hangs on a hanger, there is little or no pressing when you want to wear it.

The shirt or blouse needs special care. To avoid yellowing of the fabric, it should be washed every time it has been used. Wash your bunad shirt by hand. A cotton shirt can be washed in hot water, and even soaked in hot water for a time, unless it is old and fragile. Linen fibers are more brittle than cotton, and certain precautions must therefore be taken. Water above 140F is not recommended for linen, and if you have colored embroidery, use colder water. Chlorine bleach is to be avoided for linen fabrics. Try to soak the shirt in mild soapy water if you have yellowing and stains. Rinse the garment well since soapy residue turns the fabric yellow. Some experts recommend rinsing the shirt five times, and the last two rinses should be in cold water. Some people like to starch their shirts lightly. It can be done by adding starch to the last rinse, or you may starch it before ironing. Do not wring the shirt, but roll it up in a towel before you hang it up to dry. Do not iron the shirt before it is to be used. That also prevents yellowing the fabric. If you have a linen shirt, dampen the shirt before ironing. Turn it inside out and iron on the reverse side. If you have embroidery on the shirt, use a soft padding on the ironing board, otherwise the embroidery will look flat. The shirt will most likely not feel quite dry after this ironing. Let it hang a few hours or until the next day, then iron lightly on the right side. A bunad shirt should look crisp and clean. The shirt is best stored in a cotton bag.

Old handmade Sunnmørsknapp, (neck button from Sunnmøre), 1910-20. Contributed by Lizzie Riiber.

If you have a silk shawl or scarf, roll it up on acid free paper and keep it in a cotton bag together with the purse, cap and other smaller parts of your costume.

The jewelry for your bunad or festdrakt also needs attention. It is best stored in plastic bags with zip locks. To avoid scratches, use several bags. Every once in a while you need to remove tarnish. Clasps of course must be removed from the garment to be cleaned. Buttons may stay in place if you slip a piece of plastic with a small hole in it over the button to prevent the garment from staining. You may sometimes be told that you can use dishwashing liquid and ammonia for cleaning pieces of bunad silver. Before you use this process, you need to know that it should never be used for oxidized silver. Also, other silver pieces become very bright and shiny. If you want this look, this is fine, but if you want a less shiny look with more "light and shadow" effect, polish your silver the old fashioned way. If you have antique silver or some older pieces, the bright look is very much out of place. If you prefer the shiny look, heat the mixture of dishwashing liquid and ammonia and dip the jewelry in it. Carefully rinse and dry everything. Water spots will leave ugly marks. For very tarnished jewelry, or if you do not feel comfortable doing the cleaning yourself, bring your treasures to a jeweler to do the cleaning. If you are the lucky owner of a silver belt, it is advisable to wrap it in acid free paper first before storing it in a plastic bag.

Some of you may have older bunads which need cleaning and repair. If the shirt and dress are of a certain age and show wear or weakness in the fibers, you may wish to seek expert advice on cleaning and repair. If the moths have feasted on your costume, help is out there if the damage is not too serious. Woolen fabrics can be repaired by reweaving. Sometimes fibers from a hem, for instance, can be used in the repair process. It is less common to do reweaving on a shirt, but this can be done as well. Dry cleaners can often recommend people who do reweaving, but for a bunad it is probably better to contact someone who specializes in this type of repair. Both in Norway and in the U.S. you will find these specialists. If you contact a bunad retailer, they most likely will be able to direct you to someone who can help. Another source is the Internet, where firms that specialize in repair of fabrics, beadwork and embroidery advertise.

If your costume is well taken care of, it may last a very long time. Some people wear bunads that are eighty to a hundred years old. Even with the high cost of acquiring a bunad, when used over such a long period of time, your festive outfit becomes a great investment!

Old tine (wooden box), 1830 from Valdres, with two old headdresses. Submitted by Lizzie Riiber.

CHAPTER IV

How to Go About Acquiring a Bunad or Festdrakt

TOP OF PAGE: Embroidered collar of a 200 year old shirt from the Kristiansund area. Contributed by Ann Hougen.

For most people, buying a bunad or festdrakt is a major expense. For that reason alone you should take time and be careful in your choice. There are, however, even more compelling reasons for being knowledgeable and thorough in your selection of a costume. A bunad is based on old traditions, most often linking it to a certain district in Norway, and even to a specific time in history. As already explained, it is customary to choose a bunad from a district where you have family connections, or where you have lived for some time. If you are not so sure of your family's background in Norway, do some research into your family history. Most people will be able to come up with a district in Norway, perhaps specific places or even farms. If you have relatives in Norway, seek their advice as to what costumes are available in your district, and find out what they are wearing. Some families even have their own costume traditions. Before you order a bunad, if possible, try to borrow one of your choice and try it on to see how you like to wear it and whether you like the look.

There are many books available in both Norwegian and English with pictures and descriptions of the best-known costumes. If you have found out what districts of Norway your family came from, you have made the first step. Since many of us have family in more than one district, that gives more freedom when selecting a costume that appeals to us. Most bunad books usually show only a sampling of what is available. There are often variations to choose from for some costumes, and information about these are often best obtained in the local district.

Today there is also quite a bit of information to be found on the Internet. Husfliden and other dealers in bunads, both in Norway and in the United States, often have their own web pages with information, frequently illustrated with pictures. If there is a retailer of

Very old suspenders from Valdres, worn by Lizzie Riiber's great grandfather, Hans Andersen, born 1859. Contributed by Lizzie Riiber.

bunads in the district your potential bunad comes from, start there. They may have more detailed information than other stores. Also ask your family and friends in Norway if they have any information. They may know someone who makes bunads. That may save you both money and time. When you have selected the bunad you want, compare prices several places. Always make sure that what you buy is authentic and of good quality.

Many women choose to make their own costumes. Most costumes can be bought in kits containing all you need for your bunad or festdrakt. If you opt for this solution, be sure that what you order is a kit for an authentic bunad or festdrakt. Look-alike outfits have little or no value. Besides, you want to be proud of wearing your costume. Courses for people who want to make their own costume, are available in many communities in Norway. A few books (in Norwegian) on how to sew your bunad are on the market as well. In some areas of the United States there are undoubtedly also some help for those who are able and willing to do the work themselves. It is, however, more difficult for those who have no outside help to undertake the task of making a costume. If making a whole costume seems impossible for you, consider making parts of your costume. For instance, if you are a good embroiderer, you may save some money by doing the embroidery yourself. It is important to remember that a bunad is a traditional outfit, dictated by a long history and an accepted standard as far as techniques and appearance are concerned. If you are not capable of doing the sewing correctly, or if you choose to change certain details, you will no longer have an authentic costume.

If you want to save some money, you may consider buying a used costume. In some areas of the United States, as well as in Norway, newspaper advertisements will sometimes offer bunads for sale. Another source may be the Internet. You may place an ad yourself, or be lucky to find advertised what you are hoping for. A used costume should be quite a bit less expensive than a new one. You have to take its age and condition into consideration when you buy a used outfit. Remember to check how complete it is. Some parts are expensive to substitute. A relatively new used bunad in good condition often sells for half the price of a new costume. Older costumes often show wear and tear, and these you should not pay too much for.

Document your bunad. If you consider the fact that your bunad may very well survive you and end up with your great grandchildren, you will realize that it is desirable to have some written sources about where, when and how you acquired the costume. If your bunad has some older pieces integrated in it, it is particularly important that you document that. There is more than one bunad owner who, having inherited a costume and knowing very little about it, would have been extremely happy to obtain this interesting information. We need to remember that our costumes, in addition to having sentimental value, also are cultural objects that have great importance.

Gilt cufflinks made into a pin, probably from Valdres. Contributed by Lizzie Riiber

Cap, vest, insert and belt from Hardanger, worn by Myrtle Whitworth's mother, Disa, born 1894. Contributed by Myrtle Whitworth.

Very old handmade cuff links with five leaves floral design. Perhaps from Valdres.

Large filigree sølje, probably from Valdres.

Old shawl fasteners.

Old filigree cuff link.

Items on this page contributed by Lizzie Riiber.

Bibliography

Bugge, Anders and Sverre Steen, eds. *Norsk kulturhistorie.* Vol. 4. Oslo: J. W. Cappelens Forlag, 1940.

Bugge, Astrid. "Motene skifter," *Dette er Norge 1814-1964.* Vol. I, pp. 187-202. Oslo: Gyldendal norsk Forlag, 1963.

Bunad og folkedraktrådet. "Folkedrakt-Folk Costume." Pamphlet, 1997.

Colburn, Carol Huset. "Norwegian Folk Dress in America." In Marion J. Nelson ed., *Norwegian Folk Art: The Migration of a Tradition.* New York: Abbeville Press, 1995. Pp. 157-169.

Folkedrakter og bunader: Bibliografi utarbeidet av Norsk Folkemuseum og Landsnemnda for bunadspørsmål. Oslo: Norsk Folkemuseum, 1985.

Forsberg, Jorunn. *Draktsølv.* Oslo: Universitetsforlaget, 1991.

Fossnes, Heidi. *Norske bunader og samiske folkedrakter.* Oslo: Cappelens Forlag, 1994.

Gjessing, Thale. *Gudbrandsdalens folkedrakter.* Oslo: Johan Grundt Tanum, 1949.

Granlund Sæther, Nina. "Jeg bærer min hatt som jeg vil." *Norsk Husflid,* No. 5, 1993.

Grimstvedt, Målfrid. "Bunad - Historic Dress Style or New Creation?" *Viking,* Vol. 81, No. 7 (July 1984). Pp. 222-223.

Grimstvedt, Målfrid. "Frå folkeleg draktskikk til dagens bunadbruk." *Ætt og Heim.* Stavanger: Rogaland historielag og ættesogelag, 1981.

Haug, Jody Grage. "Norsk Bunad og Folkedrakt Nettverk." *Døtre av Norge,* Vol. 63, No. 2, (April 2000).

Husfliden. "Kvinnebunader frå Sunnmøre." Pamphlet, no date.

Husfliden. *Norske bunader.* Oslo: Husfliden, 1998.

Håndlykken, Rune. "Sunnmørsbunadene står sterkare enn nokon gong." *Sunnmørsposten,* January 12, 1980.

Old handmade Sunnmørsknapp, (shirt button from Sunnmøre), which belonged to Lizzie Riiber's mother.

Landsnemnda for bunadspørsmål. "Norske bunader. Bakgrunn, rekonstruksjon, bruk." Oslo: Landsnemnda, 1980. (pamphlet)

Liaskar, Astrid Ytredal. "Folkedrakt og bunad, to ord for det same?" *Sunnmørsposten,* January 12, 1980.

Lilleaas, Astrid. *Illustrerte bunader i Norge.* 12 Vols. Oslo (Vøyenenga): Bunadforlaget A/S, 1996.

Lippestad, Jenny. "Mangfoldighet og tradisjon i draktsølvet." *Aftenposten, A-magasinet.* No. 36, 1975.

Lund, Troels. *Dagligliv i Norden i det sekstende århundre.* Oslo: Gyldendal norsk Forlag, 1939. Vol. I.

Madsø, Laila. "Bunaden - Our National Costume." *Norway Times.* May 6, 1999.

Normann, Eva. "Klesskikk og drakter." *Bygd og by i Norge. Gudbrandsdalen.* Oslo: Bygd og by i Norge, 1974.

Noss, Aagot, "Draktfunn og dakttradisjoner i det vestnordiske området frå vikingtid til høgmellomalder." *Viking.* Oslo, 1994.

Noss, Aagot. "Festive Folk Costumes of Norway." *The American Scandinavian Review.* Vol. 53, No 2 (1965). Pp.154-160.

Noss, Aagot. "Folkedrakter i Noreg i andre halvdelen av det 19. hundreåret. Frå norske folkedrakter til amerikanske klede." Oslo: Norsk Folkemuseum, 1986.

Noss, Aagot. "Frå folkedrakt til bunad." *Festskrift til Aagot Noss. Folk og klede - skikk og bruk.* Oslo: Norsk Folkemuseum, 1994.

Noss Aagot. "Rural Norwegian Dress and Its Symbolic Function." In Marion J. Nelson, *Norwegian Folk Art: The Migration of a Tradition.* New York: Abbeville Press, 1995. Pp. 148-155.

Royal Norwegian Ministry of Foreign Affairs. "Norwegian Folk Dress, Bunads and Sami Costumes." Pamphlet 1993.

Skavhaug, Kjersti, ed. *Våre vakre bunader.* Oslo: Hjemmenes forlag A/S, 1978.

Ugland, Torbjørn Hjelmen. *Sampler of Norway's Folk Costumes.* Oslo: Boksenteret forlag, 1996.

Undheim, Reidun Gudmestad. *Festkledd i Rogaland.* Stavanger: Stavanger Aftenblad ASA, 1999.

Visted, Kristofer and Hilmar Stigum. *Vår gamle bondekultur.* Oslo: J. W. Cappelens Forlag, 1951. Vols. I-II.

Woxholdt, Yngve, ed. *Våre vakre bunader.* Oslo: Hjemmenes forlag, 1969.

Glossary of Norwegian Terms

Agnus Dei or agnsti .... A large locket or coin, sometimes with engravings of a religious nature, most often with many attachments. Worn on a silver chain.

Bellinger .... Leggings made of reindeer skin.

Beltestakk .... Costume with a large sash.

Bole .... A raised decoration on a sølje (camber).

Bore .... A round silver ornament sewn onto a costume.

Breidaband .... Two streamers attached on the front of a Hardanger bunad by the waist.

"Dalar" .... A large piece of silver jewelry, fashioned in the shape of a coin.

Dossa .... Dialect name for a skirt.

Drakt .... Costume.

Dåse .... Bunad skirt.

Fanglengje .... A central streamer attached to the waist in front of a Hardanger bunad.

Festdrakt .... Festive attire.

Flatbrød .... Flat, thin unleavened bread.

Gjæslinggrønn .... Green color made from green seaweed from Gjæslingan in North Trøndelag.

Grønntrøyebunad .... Bunad from North Hordaland with a green jacket.

Halling .... A man from Hallingdal; or a dance from Hallingdal.

Hallingdøl .... A person from Hallingdal.

Hallingkast .... A wheeling leap performed in the Halling dance.

Hardingfele .... Hardanger fiddle.

Hjerterose .... Heartshaped rose pattern on a piece of embroidery.

Høgehue .... High cap, worn with the Nordmøre bunad.

Kjerring .... A married woman.

Kjerringdrakt .... Costume worn by a married woman.

Very old handmade filigree neck button with attachments, from Valdres. Contributed by Lizzie Riiber.

Kollehue .... Round cap, worn with some Sunnmøre bunads.

Komager .... Sami footwear. Looks like *skaller*, but is made of cow-hide (no fur).

Konehette .... Wife's cap.

Koneskaut .... A married woman's head square.

Krokakvarde .... Woven ribbons, rickrack.

Kvithue .... A white cap-like headdress.

Leikarring .... Folk dance group.

Maljer .... Eyelets; or decorative buttons.

Namdalsbunad .... Bunad from Namdalen.

Nordlandsjente .... A girl from Nordland.

Nuppereller .... Tatting.

Opplut .... Bodice.

Pikhue .... A pointed cap worn with some Sunnmøre bunads.

Piperynka .... Shirred.

Plisert .... Permanent sharp pleating or creasing.

Raudtrøyekleda .... Telemark bunad — the costume with a red jacket.

Rosesaum .... Rose work embroidery.

Rundtrøye .... A man's short bunad jacket.

Rynkehue .... A shirred cap.

Rømmegrøt .... Sour cream porridge.

Samekofte .... Sami folk costume.

Sennegras .... Sedge (Carex vericaria or Carex aqualitis) used in a dried form as insulation in *skaller* and *komager.*

Skaller .... Sami shoes of reindeer skin with the fur still on.

Sløyfe .... A tied ribbon.

Spensel .... A jacket for the Røros bunad worn by married women.

Stakk .... Skirt.

Stivaturkle .... A starched, white cotton head square.

Stutt-trøye .... A short jacket (for a man).

Svartsaumbrodering .... Black (on white) embroidery.

Sølje .... A silver or gilt pin for a bunad.

Tromsøgutt .... A boy from Tromsø.

Upplut .... A fitted bodice.

Verken .... Cotton or wool twill.

Ørhue .... A cap for the Røros married woman's costume.

Østerdalshue .... Cap for Østerdalen man's costume.

Sponsors

Organizations and Businesses

Mrs. Audrey Geisel, Dr. Seuss Foundation

~

House of Norway, House of Pacific Relations, Balboa Park, San Diego

~

Ladies of Valhall, Valhall Lodge #25, San Diego, Sons of Norway

~

The Norwegian Fish Club in San Diego

~

The Norwegian Information Service, The Royal Norwegian Consulate General, New York

~

Sons of Norway Foundation, Sons of Norway International

~

Valhall Lodge Inc., Valhall Lodge #25, District #6, Sons of Norway

~

The History Bank, Museum, Publishing & Information Services, Seattle

~

IN MEMORY OF ~ IN HONOR OF

*DEDICATED IN MEMORY OF my grandparents,
Carl and Gertrude Hanken with gratitude
for their gift of family.
Like the rich threads that so elegantly define a bunad,
so too is the essence of a family woven together with threads
of heritage, tradition, faith and love.*

KIMBERLY BARDIN

*WITH GRATITUDE TO my parents, Kai Bjarne and
Margareth Thevik Berg; my sister, Kari, and her husband,
Warren Hawkins, and their daughter, Kirsten Brune.*

Also, thank you to the Rotary International Foundation, the Lemon Grove and Tromsø Syd clubs for the graduate fellowship that enabled me to study in Norway, learn Norwegian and forge a lasting link with my family's homeland.

GRETA BERG

IN HONOR OF Reidar and Gyda Einemo, parents and grandparents, and other family members who so very generously contributed to Bianca's beautiful Hardanger costume.

Her bunad is truly a "family heirloom."

Also with gratitude to Lizzie Riiber, who assembled the bunad.

TROND AND BIANCA EINEMO

I HOPE THIS BOOK — full of stories, memories, and pictures — will be treasured by my family for generations to come.

BERIT AUSTIN FUNNEMARK

*IN MEMORY OF my dear Norwegian mother, Birgit E. Otto.
The precious years we had together will live forever in my heart.*

MARY FRY

IN MEMORY OF Amanda Josoy.

OLE JOSOY AND GRANDDAUGHTER, HANNA MARIE

IN LOVING MEMORY OF *my courageous and generous mother, Signe Sjåstad Listhaug, born February 9th 1911, died February 8th 2000, Ørskog, Norway.*

AUD LISTHAUG MC KERNAN

~

IN MEMORY OF *my mother, Gunvor Eggen, who taught me to be proud of my heritage.*

My bunad was a gift from my parents along with the heirloom ***sølje*** *and purse clasp.*

HELGA EGGEN MOORE

~

IN MEMORY OF *S. Falck Nielsen.*

THE NIELSEN FAMILY

~

IN HONOR OF *Roy W. Olson, Sons of Norway, Sixth District President, 1996-2000.*

Thank you,

INGER S. OLSON

~

IN MEMORY OF *my mother, Olga H. Guernsey Cummings, who kept me in touch with my heritage.*

DALE K. ROYBAL

~

IN FOND MEMORY OF *my aunt, Victoria Skaane, who shared with her family her deep love and understanding of Norwegian culture.*

Also in love and appreciation of my daughter, Karen Seiler Sherlock.

HELEN SEILER

~

IN LOVING MEMORY OF *Leif and Emma Reinholdtsen, parents and grandparents of*

THE TUCKER, SCHAFFROTH AND HANSEN-LUBURIC FAMILIES

OTHER MAJOR SPONSORS

Esther Dyer
Glen and Carmen Hagen
Edvard and Barbara Hemmingsen
Adolf and Mary Jacobsen
Erling and Vernette Karlsgodt
Jay and Lael Kovtun
Gordon and Annika Kovtun
Karolyn Kovtun
Virginia Napierskie
Alan Sczepaniak

LIST OF OTHER CONTRIBUTORS:

Ragnhild Amble
Louis and Virginia Amundson
Helen Andrewson
Bjarne and Judy Anthonsen
Eldbjørg Backous
Mathew and Aase Bence
Hanne Berg
Ola and Karin Brevig
Doris Cords
Mary De Nino
Barbara Evje
Karin Felkins
Margaret Filius
Jerry and Marit Folts
Oswald and Malla Gilbertson
Torbjørn and Kari Gjerde
Oddvar and Anne K. Høidal
Ellen Holk
Glenda Holsbo
Jacob and Mary Hovland
Wendy Hovland-Henry
Fredrik and Margaret Jacobsen
Seth and Christina Jenkins
Lewis and Helen Johnson
Robert and Jeanette Kurz
Per and Martha Larsen
Olaug Lelevier
Fred and Lucy Leon
Kenneth and Lynn Lindebrekke
Torfin and Ingrid Lindgren
Vernon Lintvedt
Bergljot Lirhus
John and Brit Montalbano
Erling and Lydia Nyhammer
Egil and Randi Oftedal
Alf and Linda Pettersen
Siri Poehls
Anita Reith
John and Mari Rem
Lizzie Riiber
Everett and Jean Shogren
Kenneth and Ada Soberg
Sigurd and Tamara Stautland
Walter and Wilma Springer
Eva Strum
Adeline Svendsen
Steven and Caronne Van Nyhuis
Jens and Hulda Velken
Janet Kurz Weber
June N. Weller
Centes Wheeler
Jane Whitworth
Myrtle Whitworth

Index to Individuals Pictured